IN SEARCH OF
THE PEARL OF GREAT PRICE
THE STORY OF DR. FEBES TAN FACEY
As told to Tessa Schlesinger

Acknowledgments and Dedication

To my entire family, near and far, both living and deceased, whose love for each other has kept us close. To Barbara Jean Stanfield, who started and encouraged me to put my story on paper. To Tessa Schlesinger, for her patience in listening to me, and getting the book finished. To all my benefactors who helped me in my journey and, last but not least, to my dearest Lord who carries me in His loving arms.

I have thought much about the pearl of great price. It is the one I have been seeking both consciously and subconsciously since first I came to understand Catholic doctrine.

As I have gone along on this journey, I have learned many things and have come to understand that each lesson was a stepping stone to another. There were times when I found wonderful, beautiful lustrous pearls and thought that they were real, only to realize I had been fooled.

As I have written this book, my thoughts have traveled back through time and I see things a little more clearly. I wondered what exactly that pearl was, and if I would ever find it. By the time, I reached the end of the book, I discovered that I had already found my pearl and that I knew exactly what it was.

Now I share my life experiences, my thoughts, and feelings with my family and friends. Perhaps, something of what I have written will touch a chord, ring a bell and, perhaps, make a difference. If so, the purpose of this book has been met.

Dr. Febes Tan Facey
Hillsdale, Michigan.

Beginnings…

They call me Febes (pronounced Phoebe) now but I was born Mei-Mei Tan on December 11, 1928 in the small town of Virac in the province of Catanduanes in the Philippines. Mei-Mei means 'beautiful one' and it was my father's name for me.

The spelling of my name was an error, I think, arising from ignorance. My mother's storyteller friend told her that there was a famous, rich Greek lady who was named after the sun God, Phoebus. Unfortunately, neither my mother nor her friend knew how to spell it - hence the phonetic expression. Perhaps, though, it served a purpose, for no hotel clerk ever confused me with someone else!

My mother, Asuncion, was born in Hong Kong to a lady who forever remains a mystery. Susie (for that is how my mother was known) did not know her father except that he may have been a Dutch sailor with the name of Begk. An old photograph of my mother's mother shows her to be of mixed Caucasian and Chinese heritage. Family anecdote has it that my maternal grandmother was born in Guangchow, China, and that after my mother was born to her after she arrived in Hong Kong. Later she and my mother moved to Manila in the Philippines. (The Philippines has three major sub-divisions or islands: Luzon, Visayas, and Mindanao.)

In Manila on the island of Luzon, my mother dodged school and played marbles in the street across the way from her home. One day a tall, aristocratic stranger passed by and saw her. He was bewitched at once and thought my mother looked like a beautiful Chinese doll.

"Where do you live?" he asked her.

"Over there," she said, and pointed to her house.

"Please, take me there," he told her.

Upon meeting my grandmother he said, without preamble, "My name is Cayetano Tan. I would like to marry your daughter."

"When is your birthday?" Grandmother Begk asked, thinking back to a dream she had had many years earlier. In the dream, Susie married someone who had the same birth date as she did – August 15th.

The stranger paused, not sure for the moment how important the question was. It was not the sort of answer that could be altered once given.

"15th August," he said.

There was silence for a moment.

"She is yours," my Grandmother Begk replied.

The wedding did not take place immediately for Cayetano Tan was the richest man on the island at that time and it was important that the coming nuptials be appropriate to his station in life. He was thirty six years old, a successful business man, while my mother was a child of thirteen. That night, my grandmother spoke to my mother about obedience to husbands and the responsibilities of wives. She then turned towards the mantelpiece, removed the photograph of herself from it and handed it to my mother. "It is yours," she said. Perhaps, even then, my grandmother knew that she and her daughter would live different lives.

Later that year – 1909 - my mother and father were married. My mother was much taken up with her new home in Virac, Catanduanes for it was vastly superior to her earlier dwellings. It had two floors; the bottom floor was taken up by my father's offices while the upper floor comprised two bedrooms and a living room. Later, one bedroom would be used for the women and children of the house and the other bedroom would be for my father. Cooking was done outside by the cook who brought meals upstairs.

Downstairs, two clerks worked diligently at their desks, inscribing shipping dates on bales of coconut and hemp. The manager, a squat looking man, dressed impeccably in the fashion of the day, looked over their work and gave orders. Workers came and went, packing enormous crates, preparing them for shipping. My father and grandfather - Esteban Tan Goyena - saw to it that the many different transactions between shippers and farmers ran smoothly.

It was now that my mother learned about my father's family. She came to know that my grandfather, a well educated man, had a first wife, Chiwa Tan, in Fookien in the south of China. Esteban Tan Goyena had moved to the Philippines in order to establish and expand his business. Then, after he arrived, he had married a second wife and sent for Cayetano, my father. Thus my father became a businessman.

My mother learned that my father owned the concession for shipping dried coconut (copra) and hemp (to make ropes) to the other islands in the Philippines as well as nearby China. He also owned a bakery and land on other parts of the island. Perhaps, the most exciting thing was to hear that her husband's forefathers had belonged to that element of society that served the Chinese Emperor.

The downside of my mother's new life was that my father expected more ladylike activities from my mother and would not permit her to play marbles in the streets of Virac, something she loved to do. Nor was she permitted to play with the 'natives'. My mother grew lonely and despondent and so my father hired Julia to keep my mother entertained. Julia was in her late twenties and the two soon became firm friends. My mother cut and sewed clothes for her dolls while Julia admired her handiwork.

About a year later, my mother noticed that her stomach was 'growing fat' and pointed it out to Julia. Julia said, "It's nothing, just a little puppy fat." A few months later, the puppy fat began to hurt and my mother called to my father saying, "What's happening to me, Cayetano? Am I sick? Am I going to die?"

"No, Susie, be still and I will summon the midwife!"

My father turned to Julia and said, "Susie cannot have a baby wearing pants." So my father took a piece of material and sewed it into sarong and Julia wrapped my mother in her first sarong.

When the midwife arrived, she heated water to boiling point and then began to massage oil and herbs on to my mother's stomach. Ambrosia was born on the 7th December 1911, kicking and screaming, two months premature. My mother was delighted to see her. Now she had a real doll to dress and make clothes for.

Giving birth was hungry work. Unaware that she was still bleeding from the birth, my mother made her way to the kitchen a few hours later. Here it was that Julia found her, standing in a pool of blood, eating grapefruit. "Back to bed," she said and told my father immediately.

My father was firm, "You are to stay in bed and not get up. Do you understand me, Susie?" His tone said more than his words. Husbands, in those days and that culture, were like gods: to be respected and obeyed. So while my mother was disappointed that she was not permitted to feed and hold her new born child, she obeyed my father without question. She lay in bed for many weeks while the wet-nurse breastfed Ambrosia.

The second bedroom now housed Susie, Julia and Ambrosia. There were no beds. The floor was covered with soft blankets and rugs, as was the norm in those days. It was where the women and children slept each night.

Much to my father's delight, my mother's second child, Josè Tan, was a boy (born the night before Christmas in 1912); likewise, his third child, Marino, born on the 24 May, 1914.

It was somewhere in the early months of 1916 that my mother noticed that there was a facial resemblance between her own children and those of Julia. They all looked remarkably like Cayetano. She began to wonder how this was possible and learned that a father was needed in order for a woman to conceive children. She also learned that there was often a resemblance between children and their parents.

She approached her companion of several years and asked, "Who is the father of your children, Julia?"

"An employee from downstairs," replied Julia. My mother thought of the many employees downstairs in the office, including her husband, and instantaneously understood that her husband, my father, was also the father of Julia's children.

In a blind fury, she ran to my father's bedroom and tore his clothes from the wardrobe. She ran down the stairs into the offices where he was working and threw his clothes and other personal possessions at his feet, "Get out of this house! Get out, now!" she screamed.

"Julia has been my friend for all this time. You have both lied to me! How could you do this to me?"

My father remained calm, half amused. "Susie, who are you, my little woman?" There was both tenderness and sternness in his tone, as if he spoke to a child who did not understand. It was clear from his tone that he did not understand what all the fuss was about. He was wealthy and he could have as many wives and concubines as he could support.

I have often wondered about my mother's instantaneous jealousy. Jealousy stems from insecurity, and in that part of the world, my mother would not lose her place as a result of my father taking another wife or concubine.

Around him, his employees watched the drama unfold. My father called for Julia. "Take her upstairs and put her to bed."

Upstairs in the communal bedroom, my mother was distraught. It had never occurred to her that her husband might have other women in his life. She contemplated taking her own life and remembered her father-in-law's saber in the family room. She ran to the living room with the intent of driving the saber through her heart.

There she saw Ambrosia, Jose and Marino sleeping peacefully on the floor mat, a mosquito net protecting them from uninvited guests. Who would look after her children when she was no longer there? She did not like the way Julia treated children. She did not want Julia to treat Ambrosia and Marino in that way. It was in that moment that my mother made the decision to live. Her children needed her. She decided for the sake of her family to live with the situation.

Her heart, however, did not mend as quickly as her head for she did not wish to share her husband with others. Depression hovered for months.

My father, despite his initial reaction, was not without compassion and hired some storytellers from the village. Before long they were entertaining my mother with stories of ghosts and goblins, saints and sinners, gods and demons, and soon the household returned to its normal rhythm. They also taught my mother the basic ABCs and how to read and write her name.

In time, my mother accepted my father's concubines. All in all, there were four. There was Julia who gave my father four children, Anchim who gave him one, Pilar who gave him another two, and in later years, Choynoi, who gave him four.

It was Julia who converted my mother to Catholicism. (For some reason, Julia never saw irony in the fact that Christian doctrine taught monogamy and she was a concubine to a man already married.) Perhaps, it was this that enabled my mother to survive yet another shock, for my father had word from his mother that his wife in China was dying. Up to that time, my mother had had no idea that my father had another wife.

My father traveled to China as his mother had requested. He stayed until the death of his first wife and then returned to Virac.

During the time that my father was away, a servant gave Josè some juice with herbs. My brother did not want to drink it for it tasted bitter – or perhaps it was that he sensed something wrong. It was to be his last drink. He became ill and despite my mother sending frantic word to my father in China, his eldest son died before he was able to return to Virac. Josè was not quite two years old when he died and both my parents were distraught.

In the meantime, my grandmother in China, Chiwa Tan, was not content with having a daughter-in-law, and asked for my father to send her a daughter. It was not possible for my father to refuse for in Chinese culture children obeyed parents without question.

Ambrosia was five years old in 1916, the apple of my mother's eye, and it was a difficult and heartbreaking thing for her to let her daughter go. Still, it was not possible to refuse and so she packed beautiful clothes, many dolls, and all she could to ensure that her daughter would be happy. Afterwards, she cried for a long time. My mother always remembered Ambrosia and whenever a ship sailed for China containing my father's goods, she sent expensive clothes, money and jewelry for her.

My mother continued to give birth to children following her realization of her shared status, and the next birth was that of my sister, Concepcion (Connie), who was born on the ninth day of July in 1917. At about the same time, Julia gave birth to Guadalupe on December 12, 1917 and the two, born so close to each other, became very close. Esperanza (Hope), my other sister, was born on the December 17, 1919. There were now eight family members in a single bedroom: one wife (my mother), one concubine (Julia), my mother's three children and Julia's three children.

My father now built a second house in Virac. It was built of stone and concrete and there were three stories. The ground floor was used for my father's offices. During the day, and sometimes late into the evening, there was a pleasant buzz of chatter and activity that came from downstairs. There the staff organized the bales of hemp and sacks of copra to be shipped to the different islands and abroad. The second floor of my family's new home was surrounded by a balcony from which the boys could come and go but the women of the house were not permitted to go there, for it was not considered acceptable for ladies to be viewed from the streets. There was a large living room, dining room, kitchen and laundry room. Often wives, concubines and children gathered together in the living room and chatted and laughed. Life was a tapestry of activity. The top floor contained two bedrooms, one for my father, and the other for the women and children. The arrangement was a normal one for Chinese families of those days. The piece de resistance was the toilet that flushed, a first on the island! Many visitors called to see this new invention and giggled as they tried it. It was the talk of the town.

My father's house was the biggest house ever built in the Catanduanes. The last time my family visited - about seventy years later - it was still the largest house there. It had withstood storms and typhoons that other buildings did not survive. It has been used as a home, a business, a place of shelter during monsoons, and as a capitol building by the government. I wonder if my father knew when he built the house that it would become a beacon, a monument of sorts, and something that my family is proud of.

My family only stayed in this house for a few years, for they were to move to China at my grandmother, Chiwa Tan's, request. After my family's departure to China, my father converted the house into a department store and it flourished until 1929 when he lost the coconut business due to the depression. He was then forced to concede the house in order to settle unpaid debts.

China

It was a large group that went to China in 1923: my mother, her children, Marino, Connie and Hope, my father's concubine, Julia, and her three children, Francisco, Domingo and Guadalupe, as well as Julia's sister. They were to stay in China for about five years.

My mother prepared herself enthusiastically for her first meeting with her mother-in-law. She was also keen to see Ambrosia whom she had not seen for seven years. Her excitement was intense for my father had described his childhood home as a great house situated in a courtyard with many smaller homes surrounding it.

Accustomed to my father's acceptance of her, my mother did not foresee any problems. While excited, she was not unduly nervous when the maid escorted her to meet her mother-in-law. In the tradition of the day, she bowed deeply and said, "Good day, Mama Tan." In those days, it was not proper for daughters-in-law to know the name of a mother-in-law, so it was many years before she discovered the name of my grandmother – Chiwa Tan. It was considered a way of showing respect.

Chiwa Tan looked at my mother. She looked up and she looked down. Her eyes traveled to my mother's feet. There was a moment's pause and then she picked up a pair of scissors and threw it at my mother. "You are to remove yourself from my house," Chiwa Tan said imperiously. My mother was shattered, not only by Chiwa Tan's response to her, but because she had not had time in which to ask to see Ambrosia. It later emerged that Chiwa Tan objected that my mother's feet had not been bound in the tradition of Chinese wealth and aristocracy.

It was traditional for the upper classes to have the feet of girls bound when they were between three and five years old. This practice involved soaking the feet in hot water and then folding the four toes underneath the big toe and wrapping strips of cloth around the feet so that only the big toe was preserved. These wrappings were removed each day and bound tighter and tighter and tighter. The toes would eventually break off and when feet were healed they could fit into the three inch matchbox 'shoe' for royalty. The end result would be that the young woman would have Lotus feet. Those that had Lotus feet were seldom able to walk far as a result and, subsequently, they were mostly carried by servants. Lotus feet were considered imperative for a marriage within the upper classes.

Chiwa Tan would be considered a snob today. Yet in the China of those days, she was not an anachronism. Only the poor had unbound feet. My mother, Susie, was relegated to the masses of unforgiven humanity.

My mother went to live in one of my father's smaller houses on the compound and never again entered my grandmother's house. Marino, Connie and Hope, along with Julia's children, were permitted to take their meals at the big house. My brother, Marino, perhaps aghast at the injustice of it all, or perhaps a loving and sensitive son to his mother, would smuggle delicacies to her. If there was a chance that he would be found out, he would put it in his mouth, then run as fast as he could to the house where my mother stayed, remove it from his mouth and let his mother taste it.

My mother, bereft of her servants from the province, asked my father to buy her another servant. During that time, it was necessary to purchase servants for it was not legal to employ them. (The trade in servants was only abolished with the advent of the Communist government.) My father bought her an eighteen year old servant by name of Choynoi. My mother, believing that this was too much temptation for my father to resist, insisted that she wanted a younger servant and so Choynoi was given to my aunt. Many years later, Choynoi moved to Manila and then to Virac. She then became involved with my father and gave him four children.

My father bought my mother a fourteen year old girl. My mother was happy with her and she grew close to the family. Later, when my family relocated back to Virac, my mother did not have the heart to resell her, as was the custom, and instead arranged for her to be married to a local peasant.

Shortly after this, my mother discovered that Ambrosia had been treated like a servant. The reason appeared to be Ambrosia's feet, or rather her lack of bound feet. My grandmother had been outraged for, in her eyes, it meant that no wealthy marriage could be arranged for her granddaughter.

Chiwa Tan had raged to her son, "We cannot let her be seen. We will be laughed at, humiliated. We must make sure that she is well hidden." Yet foot binding had been outlawed after the Manchu dynasty had toppled from power in 1911 and my grandmother's beliefs were not current. Perhaps, it was not easy for her to let go the traditional ways.

Ambrosia was relegated to the servant's quarters and there she earned her keep by opening oysters. She was paid one penny for each cup of oyster meat that she opened. Before long, her hands were cut and scarred. Nevertheless, this did not get an ounce of sympathy from Chiwa Tan. Instead, Ambrosia's hands were wrapped in bandages so that she could continue working.

The warm love of a caring mother became a distant memory for Ambrosia. There was no more warm fabric on the floor to sleep on. Instead, at night, she slept on the cement floor along with the other servants. Ambrosia must have wept many long nights, but for Chiwa Tan, Ambrosia could never be a granddaughter. Her feet precluded that.

In later years, Ambrosia was to tell of a nightmare morning when she woke up in a pool of blood. The servant lying next to her had died during the night of tuberculosis and her blood had pooled next to her from all her retching. Ambrosia had been sleeping close by in order to garner body heat. It was a miracle that she did not become infected.

Chiwa Tan must have known that her actions were wrong for when she learned that my parents were returning to China, she immediately removed Ambrosia from the servant quarters, washed, bathed and dressed her. For a few months before my mother's arrival, Ambrosia saw local healers and acupuncturists. Yet it was not possible to keep such a thing quiet and eventually, the story did come out. As a result of her harsh earlier life, Ambrosia later developed health problems and did not live a long life.

My grandmother did not permit my mother to see Ambrosia and, for a long time, my mother thought my grandmother was angry because Ambrosia's feet had not been bound. In later years, however, she came to believe that it was a combination of guilty conscience and too much opium. She said, "Chiwa Tan did not want me to find out how she treated my little Ambrosia."

One day, feeling the loss of her daughter and wondering about her dead son, Josè, my mother visited a psychic. The shamanic arts were very much a part of traditional life. My mother went to a medium who lived a little way from the compound. She was greeted at the door by an old woman with more wrinkles than hair. She said to my mother, "I have been expecting you." She then escorted my mother, my sisters and brother into a room that smelt of chewed tobacco leaves and musty incense. After seating my mother, she asked, "Name?" and seated herself.

My mother said, "Tan."

The medium went into a trance so that she could enter the invisible world and began calling out the names of the spirits she was seeing. They were all Tans. "Who is it you are looking for?" she asked. Eventually the old woman said, "Josè".

My mother shouted, "Stop!"

The spirit-medium came out of the trance for a moment, asked my mother if that was the person she wanted to speak to, and then went back into an even deeper trance. Her eyes rolled to the back of her head, her shoulders slumped, and then she opened her mouth. Her body had been taken over by a dead spirit.

In the voice of two year old Josè, she began to speak in Bicol, one of over seventy dialects in the Philippines, and my brother's home language.

"Ma," he said, "You know the candles have already burnt down. When I died you did not put shoes on my feet and I know that worried you. Don't worry. I'm alright now and have come from a far away place to tell you to be peaceful. Now I have only one brother, Marino, your only living son, and I will watch over him so he can take care of you. Ma, do you want anything more?"

"I miss you," my mother replied in an anguished voice.

"Don't cry for me anymore because I'm okay…. Ma, I'm leaving now."

My mother concluded from Josè's words that she would have no more sons and that, if she had another child, it would be a girl.

After Josè left, the medium woke up. "Did you speak to him?" she asked?

"Don't you remember?" my mother responded.

"It is not me that speaks. I only lend my body. My spirit goes to a silent place. It does not interfere. It is the one you wish to speak to that does the speaking."

In later years when my mother told me this story, I knew that the medium was possessed, for that is what the Catholic Church taught me. Since then, I have often questioned whether it was my brother who spoke, or if it was another, an impersonation of sorts.

Chiwa Tan, discontented with the quality of her grandchildren, expressed a further wish to my father, "You are to get Susie pregnant with a daughter and leave her here to have her feet bound." My father told my mother about the conversation. My mother was not happy. So my father told my grandmother he would take another concubine (Anchim) and give her a child. The child was duly born but nobody can remember whether it was a boy or girl. My father returned to Virac shortly afterwards, for he had word that his business needed him.

My mother learned many new skills in China. She became an excellent seamstress, learning to take clothes apart, piece by piece, and cut a pattern from them. So, while the fabric of the item was often different, the design of the clothes would generally be the same. She also learned to embroider quilts and work with multi-colored silk threads. She learned something of the culture as well; that rich ladies took opium and that many were addicted to the substance, including my grandmother, Chiwa Tan. However, my mother never tried it.

Hope, Connie and Guadalupe attended school but Hope had hated it. She had to memorize long bits of Chinese prose, then rewrite it in Chinese hieroglyphics. She found it difficult, probably because it didn't interest her. She later confessed that she always developed a sore stomach just before she had to leave for school in the morning, thereby making Connie and Guadalupe late. Unsurprisingly, they were often cross with her! Yet, despite her obvious reluctance to attend school, Hope was promoted to the next grade four times within two years.

Chiwa Tan was an ardent Buddhist. The house – four bedrooms plus a living room - was built around a courtyard that held an altar. The altar held a Chinese god and my grandmother would burn incense to it. It was different to a Christian altar my mother had in our home in Virac, but then, my mother was Catholic!

While my mother and the rest of the family were in China, my father took another concubine, Pilar, and she had two children (Dioniso and Lourdes) by him. Pilar died after Lourdes was born and my mother never met her.

Three years after my parents' arrival in China, Grandma Chiwa Tan arranged a marriage between Ambrosia and Ho Sam Cang (Samkang), the youngest son of a local rich man.

It was tradition that the family of the bride arrange a parade in which to display the dowry. Each person in the parade would carry an item on a cushion; perhaps a pearl, a robe of satin or silk, oysters from the seabed, ornaments of jade or a cushion displaying a diamond or ruby. All these items would demonstrate the status and wealth of the families of the bride and groom – and the longer the parade, the richer the families.

My father, being a man of considerable wealth, went to great lengths to make it a parade that his first-born would not forget. Perhaps it was also to compensate for the lost years and for the misery she spent with his mother. Indeed, the parade was much spoken about – even in places where it was probably not safe to be spoken about!

It did not take long for the news to travel to those with open ears and itchy fingers. About a month before the wedding, some pirates broke into my grandmother's house to steal the dowry. They were in the wrong house, though, because the treasure lay unguarded in my mother's house. If the pirates had only known that the house was empty because the roof had collapsed the previous day, they might have looked elsewhere. (My mother had moved into the school house.)

Some sound must have awakened my mother because she went to the window of the school house and saw the pirates. She rushed to the school bell, grabbed its long ropes, pulled with all her might, and amid the clanging bells shouted, "Pirates! Pirates!"

Hope remembers sitting next to the garden wall, cold, close to tears and bare foot, listening to the pirates. They were angry because they hadn't found the dowry. They lit a candle in the attic and my grandmother, who had bound feet, had to call a servant to go and see what was burning. The pirates were talking amongst themselves. They had taken my cousin captive so that they could hold him captive and were wading in the shallow waters to get to their ship. They were shouting at each other that the tide was going out and that they had to get to their ship otherwise they would be stranded. When they finally arrived at their ship, they asked my cousin who his father was. He told them that his father was dead and that he was an orphan. This was true. The pirates realized that they couldn't obtain a ransom for him, so one of them hit him with the butt of his gun, and threw him into the water. In those days only fathers could pay ransom. Luckily he could swim and he managed the short distance to the shore. He heard the pirates shout behind him, "We'll be back because we did not find what we were looking for!"

This young boy was a playmate of Connie, my sister, and in 1972, when Nixon visited Mao Tse Tung, Connie returned to China to visit her family. She asked relatives in town about this young man and was told that he had become a high ranking officer in the Chinese Communist Army. He made a special visit to his home to meet with her. He had changed so much that Connie wasn't sure he was the same person.

"I'm not sure that you're the right person," she said.

"Yes, I'm the person you're looking for," he replied. "Do you remember the night the pirates took me, when they tried to steal the dowry, and then threw me off their ship?"

They went on to share memories, not least of which was trying to keep young Hope quiet while the pirates were walking the high cement wall.

Samkang and Ambrosia were married within the month and it was a very happy day, full of feasting and fervor. They were a happy couple although they did not know each other well. Then it was time to return to the Philippines and the newly weds accompanied the family back to Virac.

Back to Virac

Soon after the return, my mother became pregnant with me, and I was born on December 11, 1928. I was the last of my mother's children. After me, she gave birth to Maria who died at birth and then she miscarried a baby boy. Julia also had another daughter, Maritess, born October 3rd, 1928. Maritess was two months older than I was and we grew up together, dear sisters and friends. A year later, Ambrosia became pregnant, but she was not to see much of her son , Juanito, (Lincoln Tan Yabut) for six months after his birth on December 27th 1929, she died.

Samkang was much attached to Ambrosia and at the funeral, he leaned heavily on the funeral cart. With his head on his arm, he writhed all the way to the cemetery, a journey of some two miles. He was a man in deep despair and nobody dared to move him from the coffin, this despite the fact that it was not traditional for relatives and close friends to be pall bearers. This duty was undertaken by those of a more distant relationship. The ten-foot long cart which carried the coffin was draped in black and white cloth and covered with white flowers. The men were dressed in black and the women in white.

Samkang's sorrow was intense and he never left his house again. Each day my mother would send servants with a cooked meal for him and she supported him until the Japanese attacked the Philippines in 1941. The *amah* (nurse-maid) took care of little Juanito but after a time it was thought better if he came to live with us and so Juanito and I grew up together. He was like a brother to me.

It was only recently that I learned more of those years in Juanito's life. They were not as I thought. Juanito told me the following story:

"My grandfather hated me and treated me badly. It made my childhood difficult and unhappy. I tried with all my might to make him like me and one day when I was given some *lechon* (pork roasted over a charcoal fire) while at a friend's birthday party, I brought it home to my grandfather because I knew that he liked it. Then I saw tears rolling down his cheeks and felt many emotions. I did not understand why he was crying and I don't suppose I ever will know the answer to that anymore than I will know why he hated me so much."

I learned that some of Juanito's uncles treated him badly and that it was difficult for him to be so unloved. He told me that it was his aunts' – myself, Hope and Connie – that brought love to his life.

He also told me that no one supported him adequately during his elementary schooling years. He continued, "Although my grandmother was the one giving me support, it was not enough because she was not employed and was, in turn, supported by her children. My father did not send me money so I was constantly hard up. Sometimes, I had no money to buy school supplies, clothes, shoes, food, etc. I envied my schoolmates and friends who had their own mother caring for them. I was deprived of both my mother's and my father's love and considered myself unlucky because I lost my parents at the time I needed them most."

It was only five years ago that Juanito learned from Hope at a family reunion that when his mother died, his grandfather (Cayetano) did not look at her remains or attend her funeral. Juanito mentioned that he could not recall an instance when his grandfather smiled at him. He speculated that his mother told his grandfather that she was treated like a slave by his mother and that angered him.

In 1947, after the war, when Juanito was 18, his father came to fetch him to take him to Zamboanga City. On his way there, they passed through Manila. There, a relative convinced his father to stay in Manila and he found a well paying job and Juanito went back to school."

Unhappily, after just six months together, on 6 January 1948, his father died from hypertension. He was 51 years old and Juanito was orphaned. A distant cousin of his mother, Paciano Tan, gave him employment as a messenger at his accounting office and Juanito continued to go to school. He learned the business and his uncle helped him to start his own business and gave him a few of his clients as he had too many to manage. He also recommended new clients to Juanito.

Later, when he got married, he had twelve children, all of whom were graduates and highly successful in their chosen fields. In later years, he never had to pay for professional services because he had a lawyer, two doctor, an engineer, a nurse, an artist and many others all in the family.

So it was that even though Ambrosia never lived past nineteen years, she went on to spawn a dynasty.

Distant memories

The years between my birth in 1928 and 1937, when we moved to Manila, are hazy in my mind, and like most children, I remember bits and pieces from the past, an incident here and an incident there. Perhaps, I remember my father's importance most of all. He was the head of the family, someone who commanded the utmost respect from those who resided in his household.

We addressed my father in the third person, a formal way of speaking to those who held high position. If he asked me why I did something, I could not tell him, "You told me to do so!" I would have to answer him politely and softly that my father told me to do so. If he walked past us while we were going about our business of serious play, then we paused and stood at attention until he was nowhere in sight. We were scared of him, in awe of him, and we would never dare to treat him with familiarity. Fatherhood and Godhood were synonymous.

My father was a man of stature, respected by those who worked for him, and held in high esteem by his family and friends. Yet, he did not spank us or shout at us. He was a man, sure of himself and sure of his family, sure of his business and sure of his place.

A Chinese proverb says, "When you are most scared, you pee black." I often had that thought when I came into contact with my father. In later years I was to realize that he cared deeply for his family and that he had a soft spot for me, the youngest child from his wife.

When I was very young, my mother told me that it was rude to stare at somebody while they were eating. One day, while my father was eating *merienda*, he called me to give me some of his food. I ran away. He was bewildered and asked my mother about it. My mother explained to him that she had told me it was rude to stare at someone while they were eating. Later, my father came to me and said it was okay to watch him eat, that we were family. I never did watch him eat, though. Familiarity with my father was not something that intruded in our family relationships.

Another time, I peeped into my father's office while sneaking past his door. Inside, I saw a large picture of a Chinese god dressed in Mandarin costume. My father was probably having a conversation with the god and so his eyebrows were standing on end, a frightening expression on his face. Somehow in that light and, something to do with the way he was sitting, my father took on an ominous reflection and I, petrified beyond all reason, flew up the stairs, never to forget.

At the age of four I had my first brush with death.

It was December 30, 1932, the day we commemorated the death of Dr Jose Rizal, a Filipino national hero who had faced the Spanish firing squad. We always had a parade to remember his sacrifice. Rizal was partially responsible for reforms to the Spanish administration and therefore was held in high esteem by Filipinos. He was a man who played many parts and was just as well known for his contribution to medicine and economics as he was for his poetry and political satire. The night before he was shot, he wrote a poem entitled, *"Adios Patria Adorada."*

I stood with my first grade class on the sidewalk of the main street and waited patiently for the parade to begin. We were all dressed in white and each of us carried a Filipino flag. Always curious, I was a little in front of the group, peering in both directions, waiting for the parade to start.

Quite suddenly, a car accelerated at breakneck speed, touched where I was standing, throwing me over the hood and underneath the car. The car did not stop but continued along its way. I heard someone yell "They were Spanish hot shots", then the intense babble of the crowd and mutterings of "Is she okay?" "Someone get a doctor!" As I lay there, seeping in and out of consciousness, I felt the outrage of the crowd. I was lucky that the car pitched me forward in a vertical position rather than a horizontal one, otherwise I would have had broken bones or died. The cars in those days were built high so that there was quite a space between the road and the bottom of the car.

Finally, my teacher rushed to my side and picked me up. I was bleeding and my white dress was now a messy blend of blood and mud. I was crying, not because I was hurt, but because I was in shock. It was not everyday I got mowed down by a car.

My teacher rushed me home. "Quick! Someone open the door. Mei-Mei has been struck down by a car." I still remember those words. It had happened so quickly that it was only then that I began to understand what had happened.

My mother was devastated. "Oh no! I cannot lose another of my babies!" She escorted my teacher to a couch that stood at the far side of the room. There my teacher laid me down gently. I opened my eyes. "The bad man ran over me. He ran over me. Mama, I hurt."

Fortunately, it was more a matter of fright. There were bruises and cuts and blood and mud. My mother sponged me down carefully. She thought that the injuries were superficial but did not want to take a chance.

"Call Cayetano!" she instructed a maid but my father was at a *sabong*, a cock fight some distance away. This was the national pastime, also a form of gambling. Cock fighting was a popular sport in Asia at that time – and still is. Those unaccustomed to watching two roosters with sharp double edged razors tied to their legs in their bloody fight to the death, might not find it palatable. He would be there all day, betting his money on the winner (or loser), taking his winnings with glee and not saying too much about his losses. If he lost, we would have chicken for several meals. There was no point in keeping alive a rooster who was losing fights or so my mother thought. There was a sneaking suspicion, though, that it might have been a form of revenge. My father had a housing unit for the roosters and early every morning a couple of hired hands would massage the roosters (about fifty of them) and let them practice fighting with each other in order to prepare for the real thing. It would be night before my father returned home from the cockfight.

It was the custom for the children to give him his water pipe and a cup of tea upon his return home. We would wipe his face and take off his coat. It was my job to take off his shoes and massage his legs. So when I wasn't there, he asked where I was.

"Something happened to Mei-Mei. A car ran over her," my mother told him softly. My father got up and threw his tea cup across the room. He then went to fetch his gun.

"Who was it? Tell me now. I will kill him!"

"I was told it was Juan Perez, the Spaniard on Main Street," my mother replied.

"Nobody runs over my daughter and lives to tell the tale!" he said. He yelled for a servant to pick me up and follow him. My mighty father flew down the stairs and out the door. The servant that carried me stumbled once but did not fall. I think she was too scared to fall. My father's fury made him even more foreboding than he already was.

When we got to the Spaniard's house, my father shouted, "Come out of there, you bastard! You don't hurt my little girl and then get away with it. You coward! You are the scum of the earth!" He ranted, completely uncaring as to where his actions might lead.

No one answered the door. It seemed that the house was uninhabited. My father indicated to the servant who was carrying me to follow him as he made his way to the back door. As he was doing so, a neighbor from a nearby house ran towards him and said, 'Juan Perez has fled the province. Someone told him you would hunt him down so he took a boat and went to the mainland to be out of your reach."

The neighbor looked at my father, sympathy on his face mixed with the subservient demeanor of someone who was not speaking to an equal. "Juan is a coward and he told me that he thought you would kill him. I asked Juan why he didn't stop when he knew that he had hit a little girl and he said it was because he thought it was the daughter of a poor man."

My father returned home. He was determined to find the Spaniard and thus he made many inquiries. His past business dealings had given him an empire of contacts and he now used these. Eventually, it was the helpful neighbor who came to my father three months later with news. "Juan Perez and his daughter are dead. They were bathing in the river when an undercurrent, which had never been there before, swept them to the center of the river and drowned them. Now a higher power has seen to it that Juan will never again harm anyone."

I have another memory of that first year at grade school. I used to get home from school and I would then get on the pet pig and ride on its back. It was great fun. The pig was bathed every day by the maid and was quite clean.

Once, a fish bone lodged in my throat and I began to choke. My father took a glass of water and, using his pinkie, wrote some Chinese characters on the water inside the glass. He instructed me to drink half of it and after I did I gave the glass back to him. He then threw the glass and its remaining contents against the wall. The bone in my throat disappeared. Thus it was I thought my father not only a healer but a magician, too. He grew more awesome in my sight with each passing day.

I have a memory of a day when my father was at a cockfight and I cut my foot. It wouldn't stop bleeding so my mother sent for my father. When he arrived, he told her to pick a leaf from a particular tree. Then he wrote Chinese characters on it and rubbed my foot with it. The bleeding stopped immediately and I've often wondered if that particular tree had certain medicinal properties.

My father must have known something of the medicines of the day for one day when I lit an alcohol burner, it exploded. My face and the front of my body had a red meat and butchered look. I had third degree burns. My mother was hysterical because I was so disfigured. "I wish you were dead," she said. "No one will marry you now!"

It was not my father's point of view. He mixed powdered lye and coconut oil into an ointment, then smeared it on my face. He let it dry until it was as hard as plaster. Then he removed it by washing my face gently with cold water. He showed my mother how to apply different ointments and herbs. In time, my burnt skin peeled off and new skin grew.

My father, I discovered, was a miracle worker. No wonder he held the awe, the respect and admiration that he did.

Hope was very unhappy between the years 1935 and 1937. She had finished seventh grade in 1935 and there was no high school in Virac. My father would not let her go to Manila to high school and so she did nothing but twiddle her thumbs for the next two years.

She loved school because at heart she was an academic. Nobody praised her for the As she obtained or the prizes she won for English but she loved school anyway. She had been a bright scholar as well; in China she did four years schooling in two years and still managed to be in the top two. In Virac, she managed to be first in her class, yet my father would not let her study further.

Hope came close to suicide and later confessed she thought about taking her life. Perhaps, the only thing that saved her was the books that she read. She loved the classics. *The Hunchback of Notre Dame* and *Vanity Faire* were her favorites. The family did not understand. While Guadalupe and Connie were helping with household tasks, she was tucked up in a corner somewhere reading a book, devouring tales of savoir faire or nurturing some new interest that she had found in a book about the new discoveries being made world wide.

My mother tried on several occasions to change my father's mind about furthering Hope's education, but he was frightened that someone would come to visit her where she was staying and some harm would come to her. My mother used to ask, 'What harm?'

Perhaps, my father was only too aware of Hope's nick name, 'The little black devil'."

By 1937, when I was nine years old, my brother, Marino, was managing our bakery in Virac. Hope had finished her schooling and wanted to move to the big city. My father was not happy with the idea.

It was Marino that came to the rescue. One night, when Hope was feeling more unhappy than usual, he took her, Connie and Guadalupe for a walk in the dark. It was not acceptable for young ladies to be seen outside so the only way they could venture out was in the night air, unseen, disguised, not known. They ran into an army officer who called on their father the next day and asked to see his daughters.

My father was very upset. He told the officer that he didn't have any daughters. The army officer said that he had seen them with Marino. My father said that it must have been some other women. The army officer wasn't convinced but eventually took his leave.

My father was angry with Marino but Marino said that Hope could not sit at home all the time doing nothing and that she had a brain. He said she had to go the mainland to school. My father was adamant that that wouldn't happen. And then Marino said, 'And it would be a good idea to send Connie and Guadalupe with her because they certainly aren't going to find good husbands here!'."

It was the turning point. My father conceded that we could go to Manila and that my mother would go with us. So we packed our bags and my mother, Connie, Hope, Domingo, Guadalupe, Tess, and I moved to Manila where we lived in a suitable house in the suburbs. Guadalupe and Connie went to La Consolacion College, a private Catholic school run by Augustine sisters, where they studied art. Hope went to Centro Escolar University, a private secular school, for the next four years. We would be fetched for school by an enormous car and returned home the same way. Hope later commented about that period in our lives, "I made some friends but there was no talk of boys amongst us. Instead it was our school work that counted. I was an honors student and needed another subject. So I learned to play a big guitar and was part of the school band. It wasn't something I did by choice, but then I didn't hate it either."

It was the first time that they had attended a school as they had been privately tutored at home, as was the way for females growing up in the upper classes at that time. In the meantime, times had changed, and my mother saw no reason why I shouldn't attend grade school. I loved it and was soon doing very well.

Hope made a good friend – Rosa Tirona. Her father was a major political figure in Manila and when it came to class placement, it was she who came first. Later, she went up to Hope and said, "I'm sorry, it should have been you." Hope told her it was okay and not her fault that the academic accolades had been influenced by political considerations and that Rosa won the prize.

Rosa did not live past the war. She died during the Japanese occupation.

Nevertheless, during her four years at school, Hope excelled and won many prizes. She loved literature and wanted to be a journalist. I asked Hope about those years and she said, "It seems strange today that no one ever mentioned my achievements but Chinese people are stingy with praise. I don't think they believe it's good for the soul."

While we were in Manila, the son of my father's first wife arrived in Virac, bringing Choynoi with him. It wasn't long before my father became involved with Choynoi and soon she had four children with him.

Marino, meanwhile, was having the time of his life dating pretty girls. My father disapproved and felt it was time for him to take a wife. So he arranged a marriage between Estela, a past classmate of Hope, and Marino, who was seven years her senior. Estela knew Marino through Hope, whom she had known since seventh grade. Initially, Estela was not too keen on my brother, but as arrangements had been made, they dated. The relationship blossomed and they were married on December 7, 1939.

Connie met Carlos in 1938 in Manila through a mutual friend, William Tan, and two years later, on December 1, 1940, she and Carlos were wed. My father wholeheartedly approved the match for not only was my sister marrying a Chinese man, but he had gained someone to play checkers with and have an intellectual companion to discuss the great questions of the day.

Very soon, both Connie and Estela bore children and a flood of nephews and nieces were added to the family.

By late 1941, just before the Philippines was attacked by Japan, my three older sisters had finished their schooling and Connie and Marino had found their life partners. Hope was all set to go on to university, but it was not to be.

At school I excelled, not only academically, but in athletics. I had been tall for my age, as well as fast and agile. I was soon noted as one of the fastest runners and started running competitively but it was not to last.

My father would not have a daughter do something so manly! I was upset for a time because I had already begun to dream of becoming an athlete. But then I realized that I was indeed fortunate, for he had relented in letting me attend a public school. My older sisters had not been so fortunate. They had been tutored privately.

Unexpected journey

My 13th birthday loomed large before me. With only days to go, my excitement was tangible. Guests would be arriving with presents. The cooks had been preparing more food than usual and there seemed to be a lot more activity about the house.

The morning of December 6, 1941 was bright and I had risen early as I had heard voices downstairs. Something about the voices made me want to listen. They seemed to be urgent, whispering secrets, intense, low. Then I heard my mother's footsteps as she came up the stairs. I went to meet her, anticipating some juicy scandal. "Wives' talk", it was called.

"Come help me pack," my mother called to me as she came scampering up the stairs from my father's office. Her demeanor was anxious. There was no smile.

"Why, where are you going?" I asked, unable to imagine why my mother would be leaving a few days before my birthday. I had heard my father and my mother talking in whispers a few days earlier and assumed it was some happy surprise for my birthday. Thirteen was, after all, a milestone.

"We are going to Balete and are leaving tonight. All the family will be coming, too, and they will arrive later today. The servants have put the clean wash out on the table. I want you to pack your things in *Guama's* (maternal grandmother) old suitcase. When you are finished doing your things, please help the others."

"But what about my friends?" I asked, wondering if my birthday was going to be spent in Balete, in which case my school friends wouldn't be there to celebrate with me.

"There will be other birthdays," my mother replied.

Still upset, I asked her when we would be coming back. "I don't know," she replied.

It gradually dawned that it might be a fairly long stay and that I would be missing school. I loved school. I loved learning. I was in the first year of high school and at the top of my class. It brought respect and admiration to me and I was not keen to lose it. "What about school?" I asked.

"Be quiet, Baby," my mother said. "Here is a list. See what it is you must do and do it quickly and quietly."

I remained quiet for I knew that I could not get away with too many questions. I also knew better than to argue with either of my parents. Respect was paramount in the Chinese family. I started to pack the clothing and bedding into the giant wooden trunk that stood next to the door. Somehow, I knew that I would not be saying goodbye to school friends. Juanito and I conferred at some point and we made a pact to find out what was happening. The rain outside did not contribute to light hearted spirits either. It was the rainy season and a typhoon could easily turn raindrops into torrents of water and a mild wind into a howling hurricane at a moment's notice.

The morning passed quickly and all thoughts of my birthday fled from my mind. When the adults talked, it was in whispers. Choynoi arrived in the early afternoon with her four children, Naty, Antonio, Anita and Celia. A little while later, Marino and his wife, Lily (Estela), and their daughter, Glenda, also arrived. Marino's car was packed to the brim and there was some dispute with my father who had just arrived.

My father wanted to take further provisions and felt that some of the items that Lily had packed were not strictly necessary. Around this time, Juanito and I realized that we were definitely packing and preparing for a more permanent move. We didn't understand why but we also didn't dare ask why.

Now I started to be seriously curious about what was happening. I began to sneak around, as did Juanito, and we gradually pieced together the reason for our terse departure. My father had heard from one of his friends that Japan would be bombing Virac. The friend was a Japanese man who owned a store and posed as a business man. However, there were whispers that he was actually a colonel in the Japanese army and that he was acting as a spy. As Japan had been in a war of acquisition for some years, my father took the warning seriously. The Japanese, even then, had a reputation for atrocities. Years later, after the terrible loss of lives and great suffering that the

Filipino people endured, it was often said that my father had been forewarned and that was the reason for his timely move.

As soon as Juanito and I understood what was happening, we shared what we knew with the other children and soon we young ones were just as well informed as the adults.

Connie, and her son, Carlito, arrived late afternoon as she did not wish to leave Virac because her husband, Carlos, was still in Manila. She wanted to wait for him but my father and mother were anxious to leave and insistent that she accompany the family. Two carts had been set aside for the servants that were to accompany us and they had already departed. They had covered the wagon with some sort of tarpaulin covering but I still did not envy them. It remained for my father to lock the house and we were on our way.

Our neighbors watched the family departure surreptitiously. The car was brimming with luggage and we were packed like pork sausages inside a vacuum pack. Questions were met with evasive answers. "My family is going for a holiday in the mountains" my father informed those who asked. We had packed for Armageddon, though.

Balete, a small settlement where our holiday home was, was about twenty miles away. It was the rainy season and the wrong time to travel. Catanduanes had more typhoons than any of the other islands in the Philippines. Already I thought of the snake infested jungles and the wild places we would be journeying through. Somehow the fear that was gripping the adults infiltrated my young heart and I began to have a bad feeling. I did not want to be lost in those hills. I did not want to be caught in the middle of a typhoon. And, least of all, I did not want to be caught by the Japanese.

The roads were wet and slippery from the rain and I remained quiet for it was not permitted for us to talk. We sat and watched the rain as it became a torrent and then my father parked the car in a small clearing where a cart awaited us. Marino parked the other car as well and then the adults camouflaged them with foliage. I was shivering and wet, just the way everybody else was. The vines of the trees played tricks with the eyes in the early evening and I imagined all sorts of things, snakes in front of me, demons behind me. I was petrified out of my mind.

We walked for a few kilometers through trees, long grass, and undergrowth that contained creepy crawly things that moved as our feet came close. It was a nightmare and soon I called to my father, "Papa, I don't know where my steps will take me!"

My father, who I thought had magical powers, stepped forward. "Give me your hand," he said. He opened my palm and began to write some Chinese characters on it with his finger. "Now close your hand and give me your other hand." He took my hand and held it. Then he said, "Now close your eyes and keep walking. I will lead you."

"What did you write on my hand?" I asked.

"I am a devil!" he replied, half a smile on his face.

My father told me that this would frighten away other devils and that the spirits would not come close to me now for I was living and they were not. Now as I remember those words, those moments, I realize that it was then that I lost my fear for I was never frightened again. It was the complete trust of a child in her father's words.

About an hour and a half later we came upon the carabao drawn cart that had been left for us. It was loaded with food, general supplies and half a dozen live chickens, and covered with a tarpaulin to prevent its contents from getting wet. The livestock were not that lucky – they got drenched! I wanted to stop, to go to sleep, but there were still some miles to go before we arrived at the house. The men piled the hand luggage on top of the cart and then hooked the cart to the carabao which pulled the cart for the rest of the journey.

The rain continued to pelt down and the wind speed picked up. I thought of the servants still traveling and whom we had passed hours earlier on the road. Overhead, we heard thunder or thought we heard thunder. Then we heard planes. We walked faster, stumbling, falling, dropping things, and there was a curse or two heard from the men.

We arrived at the house late at night. Some of the women prepared the sleeping quarters for the men while the others prepared food. It was too cold, too wet to house the animals properly, so they were led with the cart into an outhouse where they spent the night. The adults decided that it had been a long day and that some things could wait for the morning.

We all slept late the following morning, chiefly because the rain had continued overnight and the morning was still overcast. Later, in the afternoon, the weather became calmer and we could note our surroundings more clearly.

The house, on the side of a hill overlooking the Pacific Ocean, was built of wood taken from the jungle and the roof was made of dried Nipa leaves. At the rear of the house, densely packed trees quickly became untamed jungle and we, children, keen as we were to explore, intuitively knew not to wander too far outside. There was a long, spacious porch across the front of the house and from it we could see, in the distance, a vast vista of sea and white sandy beaches. Yet, we did not applaud these things when we arrived. We were scared, tempers were fraying, and we had to build a new life.

It was the day before Pearl Harbor, and although we did not know yet what was to come, my father, content that his family was safe, returned to Virac with Marino. We, the women and children, set about building a place of basic survival

War!

The bombing of the Catanduanes islands began ten hours after the Pearl Harbor attack. My father, Hope and Marino were in Virac when the bombs started falling and they immediately drove to Balete. There wasn't much bombing, though, a few government buildings – to frighten us I think. Afterwards, Marino returned to Virac to keep the bakery open but the Japanese soldiers would help themselves to food, then go without paying. This, together with the Filipinos pilfering made Marino decide that it was not worth the trip to town to keep the bakery open, so he closed the bakery.

Strangely, I do not remember the actual invasion. Instead I remember the other things, the way we lived, my daily life and the Japanese occupation. It was to be a long four years.

Five days after we arrived, we saw the first signs of occupation as the Japanese landed and began to infiltrate the island. Food would be scarce in the years to come for the doors of my father's business were now shut. We quickly learned to gather fruit from the trees in the jungle and it wasn't long before we planted a vegetable garden. The care of the chickens fell to me and I kept them under the house which was built on stilts. I fenced them in with bamboo strips so that they could not get away. I knew their daily produce of eggs was important.

Fishing

My father was in his late sixties now but that did not stop him from rising at four each morning to wake me so that I could go fishing. It was a tiresome trek down the hill but he was still agile and I was his constant companion. The sea was filled with mussels, clams, crabs, squid, shrimp and many different types of fish. Soon I would become an expert fisherman, learning to milk the morning sea.

Some mornings, it was too early for me and I did not want to go. My mother would plead with my father, "Let her sleep." But I was the youngest and so it fell on me. In time, I would become proud of my bolo knife and I would sleep with it beside me and use it not only to catch shrimp, but to slice bananas and coconut from the branches of the big trees that bore them.

My father did not come into the water with me. He would walk along the beach to keep me company at such an early hour. I would take the net and go into the water, dragging the net while walking. My legs would be freezing and my toes bereft of all feeling. Sometimes, when the cold water hit my tummy, tears would come into my eyes, something that I did not want my father to see.

In another time and place, perhaps, there would have been the luxury of responding to my own pain but that was not the time and that was not the place. My family needed to be fed and there was nowhere to buy food. Everything had to be done through barter for there was no currency of any sort. Our family had to plant their own rice, corn, bananas, sweet potatoes, and raise chicken, pigs and steer for meat. Fortunately, the sea was always ready to provide us with various kinds of seafood.

We had a unique way of fishing and it required people power. So, each evening, when it was low tide, I would hustle around to find the other children and together we would follow my father down the path to the beach. Each of us would carry two torches made of dried coconut leaves. When we arrived at the beach, we would wade far into the shallow water. There we would light the torches and wait for the shrimp which, attracted to the light, jumped up.

I used to carry the lighted torch in my left hand and my bolo knife in my right one. When the shrimp jumped, quick as a wink I would hit them with my knife and put them in the basket tied around my waist. Sometimes the yield would be great; other times, pickings would be lean. Hours later, we would return up the hill to our 'holiday' home. There breakfast would be waiting: steaming hot congee (rice that is boiled to a liquid consistency) served with viands from my catch.

The sea became my home. After breakfast, I would return since it was low tide, and with my bolo knife in my hand and a basket tied to my waist, a couple of boiled bananas and sweet potatoes inside my basket for my lunch, I would walk for hours in the sea catching fish and crabs under rocks.

At times when I tried to grab a crab hiding under a rock, it would bite me with its pincers and I would bleed. When I told my father about it, he told me to take the claw and chew it and use the saliva to apply to the sore. He was probably kidding me but I believed him so whenever it happened again, I would do as he told me. Then, sitting on a rock, I would declaw the crab leg by leg and use the pointed end to poke its eyes. I would say to the crab, "because you hurt me, I will also hurt you." Then I would continue talking to the crab and say that I am sorry it had only two eyes for me to poke.

I was young and took pleasure in living by the eye-for-an-eye philosophy and it took me many years to realize that there was nothing kind about it. I am thankful that I am not like that now. Age sometimes inclines us to a different perspective.

Often in the morning when we prepared for our fishing, I would watch the deep sea divers prepare to dive for black pearls. These were uncultured and valuable. Later in my life these pearls would have new meaning when I read about the pearl of great price in the Bible. I truly understood that there was a price to pay for that precious and rare pearl. I knew how deep those divers sometimes went to obtain these truly magnificent pearls. I also knew that sometimes they gave their lives.

Weaving

My life was in many ways idyllic during that period. The lush vegetation, life without commerce, the lack of formal schooling, all added to a seamless muddle of days. I traveled barefoot much of the time, wearing panties and a one piece dress that I wove from abaca fiber.

We wove the abaca (hemp) fiber ourselves, collecting the top few layers of bark of the abaca trees that grew to about ten feet. Then we would pull the abaca strips through a steel comb about one and a half foot long. This would produce fibers (threads) and the fibers would be put inside a pestle and mortar alongside grain husks and pounded away until they became very soft. After that, the fibers would be laid out in the sun to dry. Once dry, we would divide the contents into three different heaps. The very coarse ones would be used for making fish nets, the medium sized ones would be made into different kinds of rope and string and the finest fiber would be put into a loom (one at a time) and be used to make clothes. The entire process would take about two weeks. Naturally, I used only the finest fibers to make myself clothes.

Self-sufficiency became a way of life for us all. The house needed to be cleaned, the laundry to be washed, the garden to be tended and repairs were constantly being made to the house, especially after a typhoon or heavy tropical storm. We washed clothes in the river, carelessly unaware of pollution, beating the dirty clothes with a wooden paddle on top of a stone and then hanging them out to dry. There was never a let-up. There was always something to do and without money, there could be no dependency on the market supplying us with our needs. We had to provide for ourselves by living off the land.

My sister, Hope, ever the intellectual, did not fit happily into doing the chores around the house. Yet she managed to work the system. In return for her much wanted storytelling in the evenings, we would take care of her chores. *The Hunchback of Notre Dame* was a firm favorite and many a time we would gather around Hope as she sat on her soft bed, covered with mosquito netting, the oil lamp flickering, torrential rains beating down on the roof and we kids transported by her words to another land.

I think Hope desperately missed her intellectual activities and when we spoke about it in later years, here's what I heard.

"I was looking forward to going to university in 1941 when the war intervened. I remember that for some reason I was still in Virac when the first bombs fell. So was Marino. Everybody else had gone to the farm in Balete. Perhaps, I had left with the others and came back for something. I don't remember. I do remember Marino decided it wasn't worth the trip to town to keep the bakery open because the Filipinos kept pilfering."

"There wasn't much bombing, though. They bombed a few government buildings – to frighten us I think."

"When we went to Balete, I escaped to my world of fantasy. It kept me sane. I was living a life I didn't want to live. The heroines in my books made me aware that there was another life. I was so immersed in my books that most of the war went by and I didn't notice."

"Sometimes I came out of my escapist world. Living amongst the Japanese had that effect on one. They used to put up road blocks and when one wanted to go through, they used to make one bow to them. I never once bowed to the Japanese but I do know that members of my family did. If they didn't bow, they were slapped or beaten or worse. I stayed indoors for the most part."

It seems that we each experienced the war differently for while Hope was yearning for other things, my skill set increased vastly during this period of time. I think it's a pity that many of these basic skills are lost to the young of today. I loved to sit around the fire with the laborers who lived in the huts that circled the main house and watch them work. Soon I learned how to weave baskets, mats and fishnets. I also learned to chew sweet tobacco wrapped in betel nut leaf. Sometimes it would make me dizzy but I wouldn't tell anyone that. My head would spin round and round and my teeth would grow blacker and blacker. I don't recall anyone ever saying anything about it to me.

Once, when the front door was open, just after Lily gave birth, a Japanese soldier wandered into the house and took a seat on the chair and then watched Lily look after her baby. We were all frightened and didn't know what to do. We had heard the stories. Hope offered the soldier something to drink but he declined and shortly after that he got up on his own accord and left the house. He closed the door behind him.

Coconut wine

Another love was to climb the tall, straight coconut trees. This was done by putting my toes into the hand-carved nubs of the tree. One day, while I was on top of a coconut tree, eating young coconut meat and drinking the juice, my father passed by and saw me. He was somewhat agitated! "*Demonyo* (you devil)," he yelled, "get down there! No daughter of mine climbs a coconut tree!" I slithered down the tree at top speed. My dress crept up to my neck, the skin on my legs and belly scraped off and a disturbed bee stung my hand. My hand swelled rapidly.

Yet it was my father who kept my attention. "A girl does not climb coconut trees. You are not a boy!" This did not stop my father from sending me up a coconut tree later when no laborers were available and he wanted 'wine' for himself and friends.

The young oblong coconut buds - about the size of an adult arm - would be sliced open and hung above a bamboo tub. Here the first drippings of the juice would be caught and consumed. They were intensely sweet and alcoholic. It didn't take long to become inebriated.

Normally, after picking the coconut buds and juicing them, there would be a wait of about twenty-four hours while the juice fermented to become a wine. When this was done in bulk, the harvester would attach a four foot bamboo container on his shoulder, then climb the coconut tree and pour the collected juice from the smaller tub into the container on his shoulder, then climb one coconut tree after the other, collecting as much liquid as he could. These 'wine producing' trees never produced coconuts as all the buds were sliced open and would not grow into coconuts.

Early on, I had another use for those coconuts. I wanted to go into the hen and egg business. So I grated fifty coconuts to make two bottles of oil and, ever the entrepreneur, bartered the oil for hens. Whenever the hens had difficulty in laying their much coveted eggs, I would massage their stomachs and let them lay their eggs on the palm of my hand. I became something of a hen breeder. When the hens were pretty (all my hens had names) I would let the hen keep the eggs and soon there would be pretty little chicks running around. I bartered the eggs of the ugly hens for more hens.

I became aware early on that practical wisdom and prudence worked well for me. As I became older, I realized that this practical wisdom was one of the greatest gifts we could pass on to others. If we could understand that each of our actions had an outcome and avoid those actions that brought us misery, then we could downsize the degree of misery in our lives. If we understood which actions and behaviors brought us good results, then we were doubly blessed.

Coconuts

But back to coconuts! The versatility of the humble coconut tree has made it the life blood of the Philippines. Its wooden trunk is used for posts to build houses, the leaves are converted into roofs for buildings and torches for light, while the young fruit is used for candy and the older fruit is used as a meat (copra). Coconut oil, now used globally in many ways, was originally used for lanterns. So it matters when the trees have a mortal enemy. When a typhoon hits Catanduanes, as it often does, then it not only rips the coconuts from the trees but often uproots the trees from the ground.

Typhoons

Because Catanduanes is an outer island and lies directly in the path of the typhoons, it falls victim to more than its fair share of these powerful winds and rains. Many of these typhoons are far more vicious in their intensity than elsewhere. I witnessed many and remember one particularly bad one well. It was in Cabinitan (another house of refuge for us) and Lily's new born baby had measles. There were thirteen of us and we were scared that if we remained in the house, the wind might blow the house down, a fairly typical event in that part of the world. Filipino experience had demonstrated that it was better to be outside than to be inside if there was a risk that the house would collapse.

We all ran for the cart which we turned so that it lay on its side facing the onslaught of unforgiving wind and diving daggers of rain. It was not good that my elderly father stood in the four inches of water that we found ourselves in. Somehow, he found his way to the center, surrounded and protected by all of us. I could remember that only my head was protected by the cart while the rest of my body was sticking out. There we all remained for the next four or five hours while the wind and the rain whirled cold and wet about us. When the end of the storm came, we made our way back to our living place and made the necessary repairs. It was a normal way of life in the Philippines.

Playing

Along with my family, I worked hard. There were days when I resented this. It had been much easier attending school and coming home to food that was already prepared and laundry already done. Sometimes, to get away from it all, I would sneak some live embers from the stove and place it on a coconut husk and make my way to a quiet place on the mountain and build a bonfire. Then I would pick and roast corn, sweet potatoes and go to the sea to catch a few crabs and fish. When I returned to the spot where I had made my bonfire, the corn on the cob and the sweet potatoes would be done. I would throw in the crabs and fish and have a good meal while the rest of my family had nothing to eat. After my meal, I would climb the nearest coconut tree and drink the sweet wine of the coconut bud. Then, drowsy, I would fall asleep next to the bonfire. It was good relaxation.

In the meantime, everybody was looking for me.

One day, a little more adventurous than normal, I walked to a swing bridge that connected two cliffs with a deep ravine between them. The bridge was made of bamboo strips that had been woven together to form a material-like mat. Curious to see how strong this material was and, perhaps, a little less cautious due to my consumption of the early drippings of the coconut bud, I jumped up and down. In a moment I was through the 'mat' and hanging on for dear life. I'd like to say that I was able to catch myself on my way down but it was my chin that got caught on the way down. I screamed for help. My mother and some others came running. With some precarious work, they were able to pull me to safety.

Needless to say the lecture afterwards was as long as it was unpleasant. This was one occasion, though, that I did not need a lecture. I never again jumped on a bridge with a ravine underneath.

Wisdom, on rare occasions, can come early to young minds.

Birth

Around us the war raged, furious and unfriendly. Ordinary events became life threatening. When Connie went into labor with her second child, I needed to fetch the midwife and this meant I would have to break the Japanese curfew. Curfew ran from eight in the evening to six in the morning. It was about midnight and I went along with a maid to the midwife's house. It was impossible to evade the Japanese soldiers. They were everywhere.

Boldness, I thought, would win the day. I marched up to a soldier, pointed to my belly and said, "Santa Maria! Santa Maria! Baby!" Then I made a round gesture with my hand, indicating a swollen belly. The soldiers did not take long to understand my meaning and said, "Kura! Kura!" motioning me with his arms to continue along my way.

The midwife came quickly but the story did not end happily. The delivery was tense, without much hygiene and the midwife did not boil the scissors with which she cut the umbilical cord. The baby, Norman, contracted tetanus and died three days later. Connie was suicidal. She wept and wept. My mother stayed at her bedside, scared of leaving her alone. In time, she convinced my sister that life goes on, even in the midst of death. In a country torn by war and savagery, my sister heard.

Caught in the middle

My family was caught between the Japanese soldiers and the Filipino underground. One day, the guerillas came to Balete and demanded guns from my father whom they still thought was a Japanese spy. They also wanted to know if he had a radio. My father said that he did not have guns but they did not believe him. So the guerillas slapped him in front of us. I cannot think that my dignified and proud father would have been happy with that treatment but he kept quiet and did nothing for he knew if he retaliated, that they would kill his family.

I started crying and my mother took me to one of the rooms for I knew where the guns were. If the guerillas were smart, they could have taken me and asked me, but they weren't and they didn't. After the guerillas searched the house from top to bottom and couldn't find anything, they left. They took all our food and the double-edged razors my father used for the cock-fights with them. My father's guns, along with the radio he used to listen to the news, remained safely hidden in the center leg of the big round table on the balcony where the group had been gathered.

It often seemed that there was no safe place to hide. In town, the Japanese thought that my father supported the guerillas and in the mountains, the guerillas assumed that my father was a Japanese spy. So we moved from place to place, trying to keep ahead of any that would not have our interests in mind. Fortunately, my father had four or five different properties around the island. Still, we built a small hut in the middle of some twenty foot reeds in a place where no roads led, and there we would hide when no place seemed safe.

Stories abounded. There was the one about the ten Filipinos who were in a small fishing boat when an American submarine surfaced. There was some communication between them and the Americans gave the fisherman some Californian oranges. Later, the Japanese found a Sunkist peel at the bottom of the boat and accused the fishermen of being American spies. They beheaded the fishermen.

My Catholic vow

On a personal level, there were dangers for me as well. I was Catholic and I had One God in my life that was far greater than man. It was important for me to observe the many sacred rites and holy days. None more so than the promise of the Sacred Heart. Death was a frequent bedfellow and I did not want to die in mortal sin. This particular promise of the Sacred Heart said that if I went to church to receive Holy Communion on the first Friday of each month, for nine consecutive months, then I could never die in mortal sin. So I was determined to go for the full nine months, regardless of any danger that might lurk.

Each month, I would put a Scapular of the Sacred Heart around my neck and make my way with my mother to the church. As in peaceful

Grandmother Begk and Susie
Circa 1907

Susie on her wedding. She was
13 years old. Circa 1909.

Photo of my late father, Cayetano
Tan Jong Yu in about 1922. He
traveled from China to help his
father with his business.
Unusually, my father was 6 ft tall!

Febes' family on the way to China in 1923, from left to right back row, Marino, Susie (wife), Cayetano, Concordia Molina (sister of Julia), Julia Molina (concubine), Francisco Tan. In the front row, left to right, Connie, Hope, Domingo and Maria Guadalupe.

times, the church bells rang at six in the morning, at twelve noon, at six in the evening and at twelve midnight. This they did for the *Angelus*.

Just before the ninth 'first Friday' visit, we were living in Balete and the church was many miles away. However, the distance was not about to stop me from completing the nine months requirement, especially as I had already attended for eight months. I knelt before the altar enthroning the Sacred Heart in our home and prayed. I knew that in every home, there would be an altar and that many would be praying that night. As I prayed I almost heard the words, "The Devil is creating a strong resistance for you not to finish this, but no matter what happens to you, it is important to go," It came to me that the angels would be on extra duty. Therefore I would be safe making the journey.

So my mother accompanied me on my journey. When we came to the church, there were even more Japanese soldiers than usual. They stood at attention with their guns and bayonets and we were not allowed to go inside the church without bowing to them three times. Both my mother and I, aware of the commandment not to bow to any idol, did so with a silent request for forgiveness in our hearts. We knew that it was important for me to fulfill my commitment to the Sacred Heart. When I came out of the church an hour later, I felt free, for I knew that if I died, I would be free of sin and would go directly to Jesus.

Dog fights and dead legs

Eventually, the last days of the war dawned. I awoke one morning to the thunder of fighter planes flying overhead, dogfights in the sky, and bullets dancing death for those caught in their path. It was time to make our ways to the 'foxholes'.

Some bomb shelters had been built underground for us to hide in when Japanese and American planes fired at each other. Once when a dog fight was going on above, my mother grabbed my arm and we ran to the bomb shelter. On the way there, we had to pass through a barbed wire fence. My leg caught in the sharp wire but I paid no attention to it in my attempt to reach the underground hideaway. When I finally managed to get through, it felt as if I had left some of my leg behind. We stayed in the shelter for three days and when we came out, my badly infected wound had spread to about half my leg and one could see the bone. My mother boiled herbs and leaves to clean the wound and then poured vinegar with salt and red pepper on to it in order to disinfect it. It took two or three people to hold me down for I would kick and shout all the foul words that I knew.

My family was contemplating amputating my leg to prevent further infection when news arrived that liberation was on the way and the Americans were landing. The Americans, it was said, had medical supplies. My brother, Marino, went to Virac to obtain the free wonder drug, Sulpha. However, those that were looking for a quick profit would obtain it freely from the Americans and then sell it to others. Marino bartered carabaos and horses to get some. It was certainly a miracle drug for when it was applied to my wound alongside some injections, my leg healed quickly. The injury left a large scar on my left leg but having a scarred leg was better than having one leg.

The war finally ended with the surrender of Japan to the United States. However, many Japanese soldiers remained in hiding on the island so that they could kill more Filipinos before they took their own lives. The commanding officer of the American armed forces, Hope's husband-to-be, was put in charge of finding them.

Back to life!

One evening, after the Philippines had been liberated and we had moved back to Virac, Joe, the commander of the American troops, called on my family. He was seeking information concerning hidden Japanese soldiers and had heard the rumor that my family might know something.

The family was sitting around the table in the sitting room and Joe was seated next to Hope. They began to chat and my mother, sensing their connection, decided to stop a relationship from developing. She placed a clock beneath Joe's nose to indicate that it was time for him to leave. Joe, graciously, got up and said, "I've got to go."

Hope did not want him to leave. "Don't," she said. So back and forth it went: Joe saying he had to go and Hope extending an invitation to stay. My mother was pulling her hair out. The next day my father sent Hope back to Balete on horseback but this was Hope he was dealing with: A few days later she returned to town. My sister was rapidly gaining a reputation as the black sheep of the family.

I was in it, of course. Romance was not to be kept back. So when Hope wanted to call on Joe at the barracks, I went with her to lend respectability. But I also saw that my sister and Joe were deeply in love and I saw no reason for them not to be together. Hope later said, to me, "I guess I finally noticed the war was over when I met Joe the night he came to visit us in search of guerillas. He touched something inside me. I think I fell in love instinctively and I wasn't going to let go. I knew that I would run away with this man and, if he felt the same way, I wasn't going to wait around to be asked twice."

One night, Joe arranged for a Justice of the Peace to marry them in the barracks. After they were married, Joe and Hope came to our home and told my mother. She was deeply shocked and did not offer congratulations. Instead, she and the rest of the family said some negative things.

Joe indicated he was leaving and Hope went with him. She knew that if she stayed with the family, it would be possible to annul the marriage and she was determined to remain married to Joe. So she accompanied him and they spent the night sitting on the pier talking. The next day they returned to our family home. The presumption was that they had slept together and an annulment would now be out of the question for she was now considered 'used merchandise.'

Joe and Hope lived part of the time at the barracks and part of the time at our home (after there had been something of a reconciliation). They were happily married and when it was time for Joe to be reassigned to Manila, it set the stage for the family to move to Manila.

The rifts were eventually completely healed when Hope became pregnant not long afterwards and gave birth to Joe, Jr. Later Joe transferred to Kentucky in the U.S. and sent for Hope and their two children (Joe Jr. and Marie) in 1951. The trip to Fort Campbell, their first home, was difficult for Hope, as she traveled on a small naval vessel with two small children and had no one to assist her.

There were many do's and don'ts in our way of life at that time. Dancing was not permitted for it was thought that if a young lady were to dance with a man, 'all they would need was a bed'. That's what my father would say! The corollary to that was that if dancing wasn't permitted, then learning to play musical instruments was a waste of time. So, we learned useful skills like weaving baskets, sewing and cooking.

My father taught Connie how to prepare different dishes from a butchered pig, and how to preserve it in salt and soy sauce since there was no refrigerator. Once Connie was competent at it, she taught Hope and Hope taught me. My father's philosophy was that his daughters should learn to work so that if they married a poor man, they knew how to work, and if they married a rich man, they knew how to be a queen.

Death of my father

While the war did not kill any of my family members, sadly, my father died in Balete in 1946. Choynoi was with him when he passed to that invisible place. It is a strange story.

My father was lying so quietly that Choynoi thought he must be dead and began to bathe and prepare him for burial. She dressed him in his white suit and called the carpenter to make a coffin for him. Then she left him on the bed. Imagine her shock when he woke up and asked for something to eat!

Choynoi prepared him some soft boiled eggs and gave it to him. He ate them, then went back to bed, fell asleep and did not wake up again.

Marino was living in Balete at the time and he, his wife and Choynoi attended the funeral. No other family members were able to attend.

My mother inherited all my father's worldly goods but signed them over to Marino as she did not wish to manage them. Marino was now the head of the family and continued to provide for us where necessary.

In 1973, my father's remains were removed from Virac to be buried alongside my mother in the Memorial Park established by Connie and Carlos in Dadiangas, Cotabato.

School

The war had interrupted my education. I had been in my first year of high school when we left Virac so abruptly. After four years of war, after raising chickens and learning to become self-sufficient, after developing a confidence about my own abilities to survive, I was no longer interested in returning to school. I was sixteen years old and ready for other things.

Nevertheless, I attended La Consolacion College, a Catholic school run by the Augustinian Sisters. We were taught in English and Tagalog, the national language. I understood and spoke quite a few of the other seventy dialects in the Philippines, though, for I had done quite a bit of traveling and there was a different dialect every fifty or so miles.

It was good for me to be back at school and in three years, I had finished the four year curriculum. That I was able to do so, was the result of the self-sufficiency and focus fostered during the war years. I stayed with Hope in Manila and by 1949, I had finished high school.

In 1950, my sister, Connie, wrote to my mother and asked if I could assist her and her husband, Carlos, in their grocery store in Cebu. Cebu is a beautiful island in the Visayas. Its one notable relic is the large cross planted by Ferdinand Magellan who discovered the Philippines in 1521. Connie's father-in-law lived in Cebu and was married to the sister of a local senator and was the reason why Carlos and Connie had moved there.

I relocated and began to work long hours at their store. My memory was taxed to the limit as there were no computers, no written records as to what each product cost. Not only were there many hundreds of products, but the price of each product was dependent on whether it was sold to a retailer or a walk-in customer, whether it was sold singularly or in bulk. In addition, as new stocks came in, prices would often change. Keeping tally of all this was no easy task.

I used to open the store at five each morning to serve retailers. The law would not permit owners to have staff work for more than eight hours a day and so workers would only arrive at eight. It was my role to manage the store in the early hours of the morning and to ensure that the retailers were able to stock their displays satisfactorily in the market place just across from our store.

Around this time, Carlos began to speak to me about furthering my education. Once more I balked. I had already submitted to family pressure and finished my high school. Now, another relative was putting pressure on me to go to college. I had done well at school but the world was beckoning. There were other things to do besides study.

Carlos had an interesting story. Prior to his arrival in the Philippines, he had been a student revolutionary in China and was part of the rebel group opposing the government of Chiang Kai Shek. He was caught, put in jail and sentenced to death. Somehow his father, who had some political influence, bailed him out of jail and sent him to the Philippines. For a while, he was determined to return to China to continue his work there. Then he met my sister, Connie, fell in love with her and ended his dream of returning. Instead, he served as the principal of a local Chinese High School for a time. That was probably the reason he spoke so frequently to me about furthering my education.

I was adamant that I did not want to go to college but gradually changed my mind. We selected the University of San Carlos, a Catholic University under the administration of the Society of the

Divine Word. I decided to become a medical doctor as my time during the war had made me realize how essential medical services were. However, the medical course took place during the day and I had to choose courses that were available in the evenings. The only other course that interested me was accounting as it reflected my love of business. The course was far more extensive than I anticipated and what free time I had, vanished.

I would complete my work at the store at four in the afternoon. Then I would take a horse drawn carriage - *calesa* - to the university. This would cost me a few pennies but it was the only free time that the day would bring and I cherished each moment of it. I would buy a rose, or another flower, to put before the Blessed Sacrament before I went to class each day. Perhaps, I learned to value time because I was very busy and free time was a luxury I seldom had. Lectures were six evenings a week from 4.30 and 8.30.

Sleep was scant. The courses were intense and the professors gave us homework each evening and expected it to be done by the following day. This meant that after I arrived home I would sit down and do pages and pages of homework. There were no calculators in existence at that time – only the abacus which I did not know how to use. It was headwork all the way. In those days we used ten column worksheets and, on occasion, nothing would balance. It would normally be out by only a few centavos and I would have to redo the entire exercise. Some nights, I would only have a few hours sleep.

My mother, who was also staying with Connie, was concerned about the long hours I worked. She knew that my sense of responsibility was such that I would go straight to my books rather than stop for a meal when I finally arrived home. So she declined to eat with the rest of the family and waited for me to arrive home before she ate dinner. That way, despite being driven by duty, I would eat my meal with her and then commence with my night's school work.

There were accolades that made it all worthwhile. My professors became accustomed to my work being accurate and came to rely on me. Because they worked a full day before coming to school, they often did not have time to prepare the answers to the problems they assigned. They would call on me and then copy my work onto the blackboard. If there was a question, then I would present the answer to the class. It was here that I developed my confidence in sharing my knowledge with others, the first step on the road towards my own teaching career.

I finished my accounting degree in 1954 in three years, Magna cum Laude. Not once during that time had I paid tuition as the university had a policy to grant a full tuition scholarship to the student with the highest grade point average for the semester. Throughout my three years, I had managed to obtain the highest grade point, something I strove towards continually. I had become competitive and ambitious. In all, my university days did not cost me anything for I borrowed books from the library.

The salary that I earned from my job went, amongst other things, on buying uniforms for the school's basketball players, or starting a sorority and in helping various other organizations.

Pearl of wisdom

It was during this period of my life that I first understood how little happiness had to do with acquisition and money. I used to see the unhappiness of wealthy people around me and I wondered about it. Whatever money they earned, they wanted more; they needed more; they were never satisfied. They seemed to think that their happiness depended on obtaining more money yet I was happy with very little money. It made me think.

I also noticed that those who made God the center of their lives did not have this driving need for more and more money and I began to equate this driving need for money as a replenishment for something that was missing from their lives. Increasingly, I noted that religious people had a peace, a contentment about them.

While in prayer one day, it occurred to me that many were trying to vanquish the insecurity inside with worldly goods but that it was only our connection to God that gave us peace of mind. Imagine using silver to get rid of hunger pangs or gold to get rid of thirst. We need to use the right product to bring satisfaction to the area that is lacking

As time passed, I would have little insights, thoughts that came to me during prayer. I also began to value my relationship with God for it often gave me courage and endurance when I was too tired to do a day's work.

Working girl

After I completed my degree, it was time to find work but there was nothing suitable in Cebu. So I started to look beyond the borders of the island that I stayed on.

My world had changed; my sisters were married and it was time for me to find my own path. Carlos had a close friend who was the godfather of his son, Carlito. The friend and his family owned several local and international businesses. It was arranged that I would commence work as an accountant for him in Manila. So, in August, my mother, her maid, and I rented an apartment in Manila and I began my life as an accountant.

The company I worked for dealt in cigarettes, tobacco, plywood, real estate, rubber plantations, hotels, banks and other commodities. I was in the accounting department and met Johnny, the elder son of the owner who would later play an important part in my life.

After a few months with the company, I found it difficult to connect with one of the other employees. Each time I asked him a question, he would sneer at me and mock me for not knowing. For example, I would ask him how many cigarettes were made from one ton of tobacco. He would then reply, "What? A graduate of San Carlos doesn't know the answer?" After a few months of this, I took my purse and went home. Johnny heard about the incident and sent a car to take me back to work. He also scolded the employee who was a relative of his.

I had developed the habit of studying and working hard. Those in more senior positions were public accountants and so it wasn't long before I wished to take the Certified Public Accountants exam. Of the more than five thousand candidates who took the exam in 1955, only 120 passed and I was in the top ten. The exam is more difficult than the one in America as there are four different components to the exam and all must be written and passed in one sitting, a period of three days. If one passes three parts and fails one part, one has to repeat the entire exam the following year. In the U.S., it is possible for a candidate to pass two parts out of four and then repeat the failed two parts the following year.

Throughout these years, no thought of romance entered my mind for my life was about work. During my university years I had been active in the sorority but there had been no dating. I had worked from early morning to late afternoon, then gone to school, done my homework and repeated the same process each day. Now I didn't miss any other way of life because I didn't know anything else.

With my sister, Hope, in America, I heard much about the land of the free and home of the brave. So, when a newspaper article caught my eye telling that the American Embassy was accepting applications for the Fulbright scholarship, I did not hesitate for a moment. I skipped lunch, hailed a cab and made my way to the Embassy. I filled in the application and then went back to work.

A few weeks later, I received a letter inviting me to an interview at the American Embassy. I was nervous, shaking like a leaf, something unknown to me, for my confidence had grown enormously during my year of working at La Perla. The men at the Embassy asked me many questions and I answered them as best I could. There were Americans and Filipinos interviewers and, afterwards, I couldn't remember what I had been asked. When I walked out the door a few hours later, they told me that I would be notified by mail. I was too shy to ask when I could expect an answer but was prepared to wait for months.

Imagine my joy and delight when I received a letter a few days later informing me that I had been nominated to receive a Fulbright scholarship!

When I told my family the news, they were very unhappy, especially as I had not told them about my application. It had been a spur of the moment thing for me and I had not been sure that anything would come out of it so I had withheld telling them about it. I think there was also the nagging suspicion that they would not be happy about my application. Relocating seemed to be in my blood. First I had left Virac for Balete, then to Manila, then to Cebu City, then back to Manila and now to America.

"What about us?" my family asked me. When would they see me again? What if I married an American?

We talked. We argued. We debated. I promised that I would return after I had completed my studies (an MBA). and set about choosing a university. I spoke to some friends and they spoke to other friends. In all, only names of two universities emerged: Stanford and Harvard. I applied to both, unaware that these were the two top universities in America.

A letter arrived from Harvard informing me that women were not permitted in their regular MBA program and that I would have to attend Radcliffe, which did not offer the traditional MBA. The Radcliffe 'MBA' was a one year certificate as opposed to Harvard's two year degree program. Stanford offered the regular two year MBA degree to women and men alike. So that was the option I took.

In my interview for my student visa, the American officer who interviewed me was both rude and uncouth - truly the *Ugly American*. I was seated on one side of his desk and he was seated on a swivel chair on the other side. Both his feet were on his desk and the soles of his shoes were pointed towards me (This is considered a grave insult in the east). Then, without looking at me, he asked, "How come a nice looking girl like you wants to go to America? Are you going there for immoral purposes?" I was so shocked at his question that it took me a few minutes to regain sufficient composure to answer him. I told him that I didn't have to go to America for immoral purposes, that I could make more money in the Philippines if I had that in mind. I also told myself that if he continued with this line of questioning, I would leave and go to Europe instead of America. For who would want to be associated with people like him? I later found out that he was an exception to the rule.

Hope and Joe in Germany

Joe and Hope had been transferred to Germany by the US Army and during their stay there, they had traveled quite extensively, visiting, Holland, Belgium, Austria, France and Italy. I think it was this that influenced me to plan to visit some places en route to America.

A taste of travel

I loved to explore new places so as the MBA program started in September, I decided to leave home in August and see something of the world. The year was 1955.

My family gave me a farewell party and again begged me not to go but I was set in my purpose. In my excitement, it never occurred to me that I might not be quite as prepared for it as I thought I was. I had organized an ambitious itinerary. My first stop was Hong Kong.

I would like to say that I deplaned, a confident young woman of the world, ready to handle anything that came my way. Instead, once inside my hotel room, I cried myself to sleep and stayed there for three days. The world was a far larger place than I had anticipated. I kept repeating to myself, "I want to go home." When I saw myself in the mirror, I was horrified. Swollen eyes did not look good on me. My pragmatism returned. "Do I really want to go home?" I asked myself.

"Not on your life," came the reply. "I want to go to America. I want to see Hope. I want to see the rest of the world. And I want to eat – now!"

I took a shower and then an elevator down to the reception desk. The concierge was friendly, polite, if a bit bewildered that a small, young Chinese girl was on her own. He told me that a tour would be leaving in an hour. That gave me time to eat.

The tourists on board the bus were mostly American. It did not take them long to strike up a conversation with me for they were a friendly lot. I told them that I had won a Fulbright scholarship to study at Stanford and was traveling to America. They were much impressed and it made me feel good. Some of my fear vanished. Before the end of our journey, I had developed a liking for Americans and that liking removed any lingering hesitation. It was a good thing, too, because I was now free to enjoy my itinerary.

After Hong Kong, I journeyed to Tokyo. I collected my luggage and made my way to the hotel bus. On board were some young Oriental men who were my age and we quickly became acquainted. We made arrangements to go to dinner that evening. One young man was quite sure he could read Japanese and proceeded to order on our behalf. The waiter arrived with many dishes – all of them noodles. There were long noodles and short noodles, noodles boiled in water and noodles fried in fat, noodles flavored with chicken and noodles flavored with beef, but nothing more than noodles. We thought the gentleman who ordered for us understood Japanese well.

I spent about a week in Tokyo. I went to see the Imperial Palace, then on to a Buddhist Shrine and finally to Mount Fuji to look at the volcano.

The flight from Tokyo to Hilo in Hawaii was a long one. I arrived tired but exhilarated. The trip from the airport to the hotel revealed wonderful scenery and colorful people. There was an excitement in the air that was infectious.

After I unpacked my two suitcases at the hotel, I glanced out the window. There I saw people dancing, eating and having all sorts of fun under the banyan tree. The lights lent a happy, romantic glow to the festivities and I could not wait to join them. The bellboy told me it was alright for me to go there and then offered to escort me. It was a great evening. The Hotel Moana provided wonderful food and I just loved watching the hula dances. I spent three or four wonderful days in Hawaii and then began the last part of my journey. My next stop would be San Francisco. As I flew over that fabled city, I knew that a new life was beginning for me.

After I cleared customs, I made my way to the lounge where I was met by two ladies holding a large sign saying 'Fulbright'. I made my way to them, trepidation setting in at last. They helped with my luggage and, once in the car, we chatted.

They drove to the Stanford campus in Palo Alto and then on to the home of my hosts, a family of five. The house was quite isolated and, away from neighbors, cars or civilization. Here I was to stay until the semester started and the dormitories opened, approximately three weeks later. I would pay my hosts $1.00 per day for room but this would not include meals.

When mealtimes came, the twelve year old daughter came to invite me to a meal. I declined for this was the polite thing to do in my culture. Filipino culture insisted that when one was invited to a meal, one was obliged to refuse. This would give the host time to show how enthusiastic he was about your company and he/she would then beg you to accept the invitation. After being asked three or four times, it was customary to accept the invitation and go down to eat. Unfortunately, my hosts did not repeat the invitation after I declined the first time. So I went without meals for the next two days.

I was at my wit's end two days later. I was weak with hunger. There were no shops about. I looked outside the window. There I saw some apples on the ground. I had to make a plan to get those apples. Eventually, I had an idea. My host had a three month old daughter and the family wanted to see a movie. I offered to baby sit. Initially, there was a bit of resistance, either because they did not feel that they could ask me to do that, or because they did not think I was capable. But I was insistent (hunger can give one intense motivation) and off they went.

No sooner were they out the door and down the drive, then I, ensuring that the baby continued to sleep, was out the door. I ran for the apples and grasped the first one. It was half rotten but still I took the bite. It is probably the best tasting apple that I have ever tasted in my life. There is no appetizer quite as potent as hunger.

After that, less shy of my hosts, I offered to help make apple sauces, hang diapers and clean the kitchen. So when they asked me to join them for a meal, I felt that I could accept as I was now contributing,

That was my first American lesson. When an American says yes, he means yes. When an American says no, he means no. I never forgot it. I also got to eat more often.

Stanford

Three weeks later, I moved into the dormitory at Stanford with thirty or forty young ladies. We all quickly became friends, especially as I was very much into reading their 'fortunes'. Once I told a girl who had never dated and was always without a date that she would be married in six months. Nobody believed it but six months later she did, indeed, get married. I believed in fortune telling in those years (not now for it is not acceptable in my Catholic faith) because a year earlier I had been to see Madame Habibe, a gypsy in Manila, and she had told me that in less than a year, I would cross the ocean and begin a new life. I did not believe her but her prediction came true.

We ate in the Mess Hall. The food was meat and potatoes, a western diet that did not appeal to me. I desperately wanted my fish and rice and bought a coffee pot, some sardines and some minute rice. In the dorm, forbidden as it was, I boiled water in the coffee pot, poured it onto the minute rice, and ate it with sardines. It was heaven. It also was not legal for us to have appliances in our rooms and it didn't take long for the housemother to discover it.

Many of the American students complained about the workload. For me, it was even more difficult because I did not understand the sarcasm or jokes of some of the professors. I gather some of them were risqué for the boys blushed. I kept a straight face unaware of innuendo. It was as well that I was focused on my work for the language barrier kept me working twice as hard. No favor was given for the fact that I was a woman.

The honor system at Stanford at that time impressed me. One was permitted to take an exam in one's room and simply sign at the bottom of the paper to say that you had not opened text books, made use of notes or talked to anyone. It was a wonderful system and it worked. It worked because there was trust between the students and the professors, but it also worked because the system was not abused. The honor system extended to other areas of Stanford life – like the snack bar. There were no sales people. If you wished to have something, you simply took it and paid for it. If you didn't have the money, you left an I.O.U. in the box and redeemed it the following day.

In a class of two hundred students, there were only two females, myself and another by name of Lilia. Lilia was a Filipino like me and she lived with her uncle in Palo Alto. We became close friends and some years later, after we graduated and I had returned to the Philippines to work for Johnny, I invited her to come work for me.

There I trained her and when I left Johnny for a second time and he asked me who would do my work, I pointed to Lilia and said, "She will. I have trained her and have even taught her some Chinese." In later years, Lilia married and became very rich through Johnny. She never left the Philippines again.

The coursework was intense: ninety six credit hours or six quarters at sixteen credit hours per quarter for an MBA. There were no elective courses and for four days a week, we focused on academia. The fifth day was reserved for field trips to research various case studies.

One particular field trip comes to mind. It was to a bank in San Francisco. There were about sixty of us and although our names were sent in advance, the host did not realize that there would be a female within the group (me)! Management duly welcomed us and we were escorted into the elevator. I was soon aware that I was being stared at and I felt uneasy. That uneasiness increased as the elevator neared the top floor.

I checked to see if my slip was showing, then glanced quietly at my legs to see if there was a run in my stockings. Nothing. I glanced in the mirror to see if there was something on my face. No, my face was clean. The elevator stopped at the top floor and we all stepped out into the lobby. There I observed the executives who had come to meet us. They were talking softly amongst themselves. Finally I knew what it was all about.

Two VPs explained to me that it was a male only area. (It was unusual in those years for a woman to do an M.B.A., although today, the MBA program at Stanford is about half and half.) The executives offered me two choices. Either they could take the entire class out to lunch somewhere or they could take me to any restaurant of my choice in San Francisco. It seemed to be a bit extravagant to haul the entire class out for lunch when it had already been prepared so I indicated that I would be happy to dine with them. We went to the St. Francis Hotel and I had a great time.

I was often the envy of the women in my dorm. They battled to get dates. I had too many. It was a nice place to be and I was grateful for it. I ate in the mess hall about a quarter of the time because the boys often fed me. Sometimes, they would bring extra sandwiches and other times they would invite me for dinner.

I think that this was misinterpreted by the Dean's secretary, Miss Remele, who thought that I might not have enough money for food and insisted that I take a loan. Despite my explanation that I did have sufficient money, she was determined that I should take a loan. Not knowing how to refuse, I accepted the loan for a few hundred dollars and paid it back the following month without her knowing about it. We were both happy with the arrangement. I didn't owe anyone any money and the secretary felt good because she had assisted a foreign student.

In the summer, I worked for two weeks for a Mr. Melcher in order to buy a bicycle. Mr. Melcher was the brother of the man who was married to film star, Doris Day. When the two weeks were up and I had earned enough to buy the English bicycle I wanted, I tendered my resignation. Mr. Melcher did not want me to go and offered me an increase in salary to stay but I had classes ahead of me.

Initially, I did not accept dates while at Stanford and if asked, would simply say, "Because I don't go out on dates." However, as I became accustomed to the American way of life, this changed.

There was a professor at Stanford whom I had met earlier in the Philippines. He was in his mid-fifties, divorced with three grown children and he began to take me under his wing. He taught me to ride a bike and drive a car. Sometimes, after these activities, we would go to his house and cook dinner. Then we would sit by the fire and talk. Perhaps, he impressed me because he was a close friend of Robert Frost, the poet, and he would read me his poems while we were seated by the fireplace. Afterwards he would take me back to my dorm. It was now that I had my first thoughts of marriage and so, when he asked me to marry him shortly before I graduated, I accepted. I explained to him that he would have to come to the Philippines to seek permission from my family to marry me and that I would be spending six months traveling before I returned home.

By going to summer school, I graduated within eighteen months rather than the normal two years. With the money I saved by not buying food, I was once more able to have a holiday and do some traveling on my way home. It was a six month vacation that I shall never forget.

Seeing the world

My first port of call was New York and I spent a few days there. Then I traveled to London which was then very much a world capital as it was the center of the British Empire. My next stop was Greece.

Unlike London, there were not many Chinese restaurants in Greece and so I stopped someone on the street to ask him where I could find a

Chinese eatery. He couldn't speak English. Then I stopped someone else and then someone else. Eventually, there was an entire group around me and not one of them spoke English. Then, finally, one did. I asked him where there was a Chinese restaurant. He guided me there and the entire group followed me like a parade. When I took my seat next to the window and looked out, there they were - all were waving at me. I waved back, and smiled, careful that I did not spill some food.

Then it was on to Italy. There I visited Sorrento. I stayed at an hotel on a cliff. It was so beautiful that I promised myself that one day when I was on my honeymoon, this would be the place that I would come. Thereafter it was Switzerland.

My next stop was the Middle East and I visited Lebanon. At one point, I wanted to see Damascus and joined the hotel tour to visit Syria. When I arrived at the border, I was not permitted through because I had a Filipino passport and needed a visa. I guess they assumed that all the tourists at the hotel were American citizens and they did not need a visa. So, I was left at the border and waited for Providence. Soon it arrived in the shape of a truck with two men inside. I wrote Beirut with a question mark on a piece of paper and they nodded. They let me sit between the two of them and as we passed through the mountains, the two of them would look at each other and smile. I smiled back at them and I was never afraid although they could have raped me or murdered me. Then I wrote the name of my hotel and they took me there and they did not even accept money. They were nice men.

Then came Calcutta in India. I stayed in a nice hotel but when the chef brought me food, the flies followed him from the kitchen. I wondered what the kitchen was like and didn't eat at the hotel for my entire stay in India. I bought fruit and drank soda pop. The streets weren't very nice either. They smelled of cow dung as cows were not allowed to be slaughtered because they were sacred.

Mother Teresa was in Calcutta at that time. She picked up the dying men or women who lay in the gutters of the smelly streets and then took them to a house where she and other nuns would clean them up, feed them and hold them. The last thing these people knew before they died, was that someone loved them. Somebody mentioned to Mother Teresa that there were so many old and broken people dying in the streets that it was not possible to take care of them all. She said she could take care of one and then another, and after that a third, and in that way, she could do what was possible for her to do. I mention this because I left Calcutta after a few days since I could not stand the filth. Mother Teresa saw humanity inside those bodies and ignored the filth. She deserved to become a saint! And she is!

While I was traveling, I would pack my dirty clothes in a parcel and instruct the concierge at the hotel to mail the package to Manila in a month or so, so that it did not arrive before me. My family did not know that I was traveling and I did not want to have to answer any awkward questions. By the time I got back to Manila, my suitcases were filled with souvenirs and I did not have any clothes to wear. So, when I arrived home, my mother hired a couple of dressmakers to sew some dresses for me since there were many parties to attend. In Manila, at that time, there were no ready made dresses that you could buy in a department store. It was good to be home again!

Missed marriage

Upon my arrival back in the Philippines, I went to see my Father Confessor, an American priest. I told him that I would be marrying an American professor. To my astonishment, he offered no happy words of congratulations but was outraged.

"How can you marry a man who is divorced, a man who is twice your age? You are Catholic! This is not acceptable." He asked me for the name and address of the man I intended to marry and, unbeknown to me, he wrote to him. Not too many weeks later, I received a letter from the professor telling me that the priest had written to him and had told him to leave me alone. "This will be my last letter to you." He wrote, "It is like someone whose back is all taped up and when you want to remove the tape you do not peel it little by little. Instead, you peel off a corner and rip it off. You will scream from the pain but it is all over at one time – instead of prolonging the agony."

I was hysterical. I made my way to the rectory where Father Bunzel lived and yelled at him, "I will never forgive you! I hate you! I hate you! I hate you!" The priest said nothing, just listened patiently to my tirade. Afterwards, having said my piece, I made my way home, not much happier.

To skip ahead, many years later, my confessor, Father Bunzel, retired in Chicago at the Mother House and he requested me to visit him as he wished to meet Ed. After that, Ed and I would visit him occasionally and he even came to Hillsdale to visit us. Some years later, we had a phone call from the Father Rector saying that Father Bunzel had died. On sorting through the priest's drawers, he had found a piece of paper saying that if anything happened to him, I was to be informed.

Perhaps, no one remembers Father Bunzel now but I remember him telling me that he was a prisoner of war during the Japanese occupation in Manila as he was an American. As a result of the conditions in camp, he eventually weighed about 100 lbs and as a 6' tall man, he had about a week to live. He could not even sit up for his bones would stick out of his skin if he did so. The Americans arrived in the nick of time and he was given medical treatment. He later wrote a book about his time in the Japanese concentration camp which was situated at the Santo Tomas University in Manila.

Back to Business
The year was 1957.

Once more, I took a position with Johnny, this time as an international consultant. I traveled all over the world, met presidents of corporations and then examined their accounts and reported to Johnny.

When I arrived I was usually met by the president of the company, then checked into a first class hotel and afforded every courtesy. There were also some unusual aspects.

It was the custom that when wives accompanied husbands, the wives would be given a bag of local currency to go shopping. When I arrived, there was some confusion. I was an executive but I was also a woman. What to do? They would dutifully give me the bag of local currency to cover both contingencies, but before I left the country, I would return the bag of money intact.

Perhaps my life would have been regarded as glamorous by some; for it took me to many exotic places. Johnny was planning to build a hotel in Taipei and although it would be some years before it came to fruition, there was always the thrill of new investment and the challenge of current big business.

It was at this time that I first visited the rubber plantation in Borneo. An island in Sarawak was owned by the company. It included an airfield plus barges that ferried the sap from the rubber trees to customers in China, our chief client.

The people on this island were happy. They had no telephones and no televisions. They worked - or didn't work - at the rubber plantations. Their long houses, built of bamboo and nipa leaves, housed three or four families who shared a kitchen. The bathrooms were outside.

I spent one fascinating month on this island in which I learned about rubber. My first tour through one of the plantations was accompanied by a manager and two islanders. We drove in a jeep through heavy foliage and after a ten minute drive arrived at the foreman's bamboo cabin.

The tall trees with large, dark green leaves were fragrant and beautiful. They had been growing for many years and I never did establish the origins of the plantation. Vaguely, I remembered a story of *Hevea* seeds that were originally cultivated at Kew Gardens in England and which had made their way to Borneo. Certainly, the trees I saw were adult trees, not saplings, although I recall that the saplings I did see, were grafted rather than grown from seed.

The trees produced a white sap which was collected in two ways. In one, islanders would cut into the bark and let the sap (latex) drip into containers. In the other, the trees would be felled and then the sap would be removed. Once the sap was removed, it would stand for a few days and turn into a dirty white substance.

The containers would then be assembled in a large bamboo outbuilding and there it would be hosed with hot water until it was clean. It did look whiter after this process but not much. Then it was taken to another outbuilding on a different part of the island and here it was boiled in enormous vats. Once it was cooled, it would be shaped into large blocks and then prepared for shipping to our clients. The islanders would load them onto large trucks and these would be driven down to the harbor, and then they would be shipped and the process would begin all over again.

I learned quite a bit about rubber lore while on the island. Up to that time, I had been unaware that rubber was edible and that the tribes of South America used it for its healing properties. Or that there were many species of rubber trees and that this tropical tree grew naturally in South America (our biggest competitor), India, Malaysia, Trinidad, and even Africa.

By far the biggest surprise, though, was that chewing gum was produced from rubber trees. I discovered that the ancient Greeks, Native Americans, and the Mayans all chewed gum! In ancient times, it was chewed straight from the trees but production today is more sophisticated and sugar and flavor are added.

From a financial point of view, the history of rubber was also fascinating. Rubber became a highly desirable commodity when the car was invented at the end of the 19th century. At that point, Brazil had been the prime source of rubber and the Rubber Barons, wealthy rubber entrepreneurs, were born. They were responsible for Manaus, a garrison town founded in the 17th century by the Portuguese, becoming the world center of the rubber trade at that time. There were many stories about the Rubber Barons. Their wives didn't like the water of the Amazon and so they sent their dirty laundry to Europe by ship to be washed there. Enormous palaces were built and furnished with the most exclusive furniture of the day. They used gold coins as currency and let their horses drink from silver buckets filled with champagne.

At the time that I was working for Johnny, the rubber market had not yet been supplanted by plastic products and the plantations were immensely profitable.

Each time I returned to Manila from a business trip, I would be happy to be home. Each time I went out into the field, a bubble of excitement would overwhelm me as I became more and more acclimatized to living in an international world.

Connie and Culinary

It was during this time that Connie and I saw a great deal of each other and I used to delight in the stories she told me.

Of particular interest were the many fascinating culinary dishes of the east. Some methods were truly gory. Peking duck, for instance, was prepared very differently in America to the way it was in Beijing. In order to get a better taste, the duck was force fed the last few days of its life by inserting a tube down its throat and pouring food down it.

Connie would go, along with her husband and friends, to the Wild Life Restaurant in Hong Kong. Here they sat around a table with a lazy susan at its center. Next to them, alongside a wall with long poles attached, were chained live monkeys. Patrons would order these monkeys to eat. The monkey would then be shaved and the top of the head would be sawed off without causing any impairment to the brain. The top of the head would be put on the monkey again, much as a lid to a container. Then the monkey would be tied up and be seated on the hot plate underneath the lazy susan. Thereafter, the switch would be turned on and the monkey would jump! The patrons would take the 'lid' off the monkey and spoon out the brains to eat.

Yet another dish popular in Hong Kong was the Drunken Shrimp. The chef would wheel along a trolley with a basin full of live shrimp. The patrons seated around the table would see the chef pour whiskey over the shrimps, then set them alight and the shrimps would jump and finally turn red when they were cooked. (The shrimps absorbed sufficient whiskey for the dish to be known as Drunken Shrimp.) The chef would dish out the shrimps, putting two on each plate, and the patron would peel and eat them, and as they ate the shrimps, imbibe whiskey.

Connie's favorite dish was less dramatic. It entailed covering a spiced chicken with clay. It would rest all day covered in this mud. In the evening, it would be baked in the mud. When it was ready to be served, the chef would bring it along to the table and there he would take a hammer and lightly tap it. The clay would fall off, revealing a very, very succulent chicken inside. She told us that it had an unrivalled taste. This dish was called Beggar Chicken.

One Chinese New Year's eve, Connie and Carlos gave a party and invited some high ranking Chinese government officials. One of the appetizers was served from a container the size and shape of a four foot boat. It was filled with crushed ice and lobsters. Only the premium parts of the lobster were used and these were cut into one inch square pieces. The lobster had been imported from Australia and was quite expensive but the Chinese do not skimp when it comes to food. They have the most exotic taste in the world and their food arrangements are exceptionally artistic.

Mankind

Between the years 1957 and 1960, Lilia and I would often go out at night to one of the top restaurants in Manila. One evening, an older man was sitting across the way from us and he came to speak to us. He asked us what we wished to eat and told us he would prepare the food for us personally. I recognized the man because he was an important city dignitary and so did not believe that he would get his hands dirty by cooking. However, he left our table, made his way to the kitchen and came back with our order about ten minutes later. We were astounded.

Later I went to the restroom and while I was gone, he asked Lilia where I worked. She told him that we were both employed by La Perla and when I came back to the table, he was leaving. About a week later, I glanced out of my office window and saw the sleek black

Mercedes with its city number plate enter the company gates. Out stepped the well known man. He had come to see me!

After that, he called every few days and it became embarrassing. Johnny, too, was becoming angry and jealous. "I understand that you are a woman and wish to marry and have children," he said to me. "I will marry you. I love you and need you."

"But Johnny," I said, "you are already married."

Johnny already had two wives and I would be wife number three. I thought back to the wives and concubines of my father and I thought back to my experiences in America, and to my widening grasp of other cultures (as a result of extensive travel). I was no longer able to accept polygamy and the thought of sharing a husband with concubines was anathema to me. So while my boss professed love and an important city dignitary was infatuated with me, I could not take it seriously.

New York

It was partially this pressure that made me return to America (that - and the fact that I was now considering studying for a PhD). I was determined to be married to a man who only had one wife – me! I found it uncomfortable to live with the unfolding situation and it was difficult to explain this in a culture where married men pursued *available* women legitimately. I tried to explain that I did not want to be a second wife or a third wife or a concubine. It did not help.

Eventually, in the early months of 1960, I made a decision to leave La Perla and applied to New York University to pursue a doctorate. Then I set about finding a scholarship and was fortunate in that I received both the Lincoln and the Ford Foundation scholarships. This, together with the money I had saved, would make it financially possible for me to live in New York for the full four years I needed to be there to complete my doctorate. I now only needed a sponsor to accommodate American law. Johnny asked Mr. Walter Ruthenburg, a tobacco supplier to La Perla, whose office was in Wall Street, to sponsor me.

This time I told my mother, my relatives and my friends that I could not commit to returning. Nor could I promise that I would not marry an American. In no time at all, I was on my way to New York and to a new life.

I arrived in New York in the early afternoon, a few weeks before school started. I checked into a hotel on Eighth Street that the school had reserved for me. When I checked in, there was a Chinese woman in the lobby so we talked for a while and she invited me to stay with her since she had an apartment. I gracefully declined her offer because I told her that if anyone would look for me, New York University would refer them to this hotel. After I checked into my room and unpacked my suitcases, I lost no time in finding a cab to take me to Broadway. The city was a shock to the senses. Vibrant, colorful and ever busy, it appealed to me on every level.

There I saw a show called, *"Flower Drum Song"*. I loved it because the show had a Chinese background. It was wonderful and I enjoyed it very much. It was eleven in the evening before I arrived back in my room.

The phone rang almost as I arrived. It was a man's voice and it said, "Hi, Baby." Although I didn't recognize the voice and couldn't think who it was, I thought it must be a friend. Who else would know my nickname? He continued, "Baby, can I see you in five minutes?" I said yes. Five minutes later there was a knock at the door. I left the chain on and opened the door as far as the chain would allow. It was an American man.

I asked him who he was. "That's not important," he replied. "I want to have a good time." Then he showed me a lot of money. I looked at him and said, "I have a lot of money, too. Please leave." Then I shut the door and called the receptionist downstairs to ask how it was possible for someone to know my phone number and my room number when I had only just arrived in New York. The receptionist said she did not give out any information. This puzzled me for some time until a few months later, I stopped at a restaurant on Eighth Street and noticed that the bartender was the same Chinese girl that I met in the lobby of the hotel when I had checked in. Suddenly, it all made sense. No doubt one of her patrons had asked if she knew anyone and she had offered my name and other information for a tip!

A few weeks later I moved into a dormitory at New York University in Washington Square and stayed there for a year. However, I found it restrictive as there were time limits to how long friends could stay, and they could only be entertained in the common room, rather than in our own rooms. So, I began to look for an apartment.

I found a lovely apartment in the heart of Manhattan – on the corner of 14th Street and 5th Avenue. As I had a scholarship, substantial savings from my years working for Johnny, and an income from grading bluebooks for some professors, I was well able to afford the rent. I was also able to see most Broadway shows on opening nights.

Once more, the female students in my chosen field were outnumbered by the male students. It was bliss on wheels for I was never short of boyfriends. One day, quite unexpectedly, four boyfriends arrived within fifteen minute intervals of each other at my apartment. I sat them down with a game and while they played *Parchessi*, I provided the food and drinks. Eventually, they all left.

Of course, it also meant that, like my time at Stanford, I seldom had to worry about meals as there was always a friend to invite me to some new restaurant or even to a cozy snack bar down the road. I had a boyfriend who took me running and a boyfriend who took me to Broadway, a boyfriend to take me to dine out and a boyfriend to take me to lectures. They were great times.

Studying with Dr. von Mises

Yet my purpose in coming to New York University was not to socialize; it was to obtain my doctorate.

I chose my subjects wisely as I needed sixty credit hours to satisfy the PhD requirements since I already had an MBA. Naturally, I chose those subjects that I knew something about. A foreign language was a prerequisite so I took Spanish since I had taken some Spanish in high school and college. I could therefore be assured that there would not be quite as much studying to do. My major fields of study were economics, marketing, accounting, investments, money and banking, and finance.

One of my most fascinating classes was with Dr. Ludwig von Mises, the founding father of Austrian economics. I had heard about Dr. von Mises through Edward Facey who was one of my classmates in economics. Edward was very keen to study under this professor and very serious about his work, as was I, so I decided to take this class as well.

On my first day in class, we were seated around a long conference table and I happened to sit across from Dr. von Mises. He asked a question, "What do you when you are indifferent?" He pointed to me and said, "You!"

I said, "Who? Me?"

"Yes, you," he said.

I shrugged my shoulders and said, "Nothing."

Dr. von Mises was very satisfied with my answer. He said, "Of course, when you are indifferent, you don't do anything." He thought I was very smart.

Dr. von Mises was a dynamic teacher. I was fascinated by his classes and found that the more he taught us, the more avenues it opened for me. I had many questions and, reluctant to interrupt in class, I would place a 3" by 5" card on his desk with a question before class. He would pick up the card, look at me, and then answer the question. Needless to say, he recognized my writing even without my name.

Dr. von Mises taught Laissez Faire economics; Keynesian principles were not something he agreed with. I learned much from him and there was a good interaction between us. I bathed in the warm feeling of respect that he gave me. When I met with him in his office, he would stand up, take my coat and hang it and then he would take my hand and kiss it. I think I held a very special place in Dr. von Mises' heart.

He would invite students to his apartment for 'high tea', a sort of early supper that is traditional in some parts of Europe and England. Edward and I attended on many occasions. We discussed the economic issues of the day and, no doubt, Edward and I picked up as much there as we did in class.

At the end of the semester, it was the norm for his class to write a term paper since he did not give a test. I asked Dr. von Mises if I had to write a term paper (to write a term paper the student has to read his books, for example, "Human Action" which was over 800 pages). I would read a few pages and fall asleep. How could I write a term paper? So when he said that I did not need to write a term paper because I "had said enough", I was in seventh heaven and he gave me an A- for the course.

Edward and I continued to go to the many suppers at the von Mises and heard many interesting stories about the great man. He was often awarded prizes and his wife, Margit, told me a story about one of those occasions. Her husband was getting on in years (in his early eighties), and he was on his way to collect an award. En route, he discovered that he did not have his dentures. He discovered this when his wife asked him a question and he opened his mouth to reply and discovered an indistinct flow. There was no time to return home to fetch his dentures so when Dr. von Mises arrived on the podium, he took his prize, nodded his head, and made his way back to his seat. Never was a man more silent.

Dr. von Mises was honored several times during my years at New York University. In 1962, he was awarded the Austrian medal of honor for science and arts in recognition of his *'distinguished activities as a scholar and teacher and for his internationally recognized work in the fields of political science and economics'*.[1] In 1963, he was awarded an honorary *'Doctorate of Laws'* degree by New York University for *his exposition of the philosophy of the free market, and his advocacy of a free society.'*[2] And in 1964, shortly after I graduated, he was awarded another honorary degree; this time a Doctorate of Political Science by the University of Freiburg, Breisgau, Germany.

Recreation

Gradually, I acclimatized to the American way of doing things. If I worked hard, then I played hard and had many boyfriends. One of these was with a young lad of Irish extraction by name of Tom. He was very handsome and worked as an understudy for various shows in Broadway. Tom also dabbled in advertising. It was his interest in advertising that brought about our introduction to each other in our Spanish class.

Tom observed my hands and said they were beautiful and I had great nails. He asked me if I would pose for photographs as my hands could be used for advertising. While I wasn't too keen on this, I did find him attractive and easy going and when he invited me to an opening night at a Broadway theatre, I did not decline. It was a wonderful, exciting evening, and the start of many more Broadway dates. In the years that I dated Tom, I think I saw most of the Broadway productions.

Tom was a romantic at heart and each night he took the train home to New Jersey. En route, he would compose a poem for me and the following morning arrive with some flowers picked from his mother's garden. He would drop the flowers and the poem off at the housemother's desk for me. It was exciting and the other girls envied me.

Yet, there was doubt in my mind about Tom. He told me that his aunt was in a mental asylum and that his sister had had a nervous

[1] http://www.mises.org/content/mises.asp
[2] http://www.mises.org/content/mises.asp

breakdown. I often wondered if the same thing would happen to him. Tom had such a soft heart and loved me a little too passionately for comfort.

Tom would also take me dancing at exclusive clubs where well known artists would perform. I always remember Chubby Checker who, at that time, had more than twenty top-forty hits. Tom was a good dancer but as a result of the Chinese attitude about dancing, it was not something I did. So I sat out while the many girls who found my good looking escort highly desirable, danced with him. I would sit on my chair, immersed in watching a world famous man perform. It is an experience that I have never forgotten.

The New York of the 60s was a place of many different experiences and I heard many stories. One night Tom worked late and missed his train home to New Jersey. He accepted an invitation to stay with his boss overnight. Midway through the night, Tom awoke to find his boss asleep next to him. He jumped out of bed, dressed as fast as he could, then walked to Washington Square Park and spent the rest of the night on a bench.

Tom proposed to me fairly early on but I wasn't ready to get married. He offered his class ring to me. I could not take it and explained to him that I was not ready to get married and to make choices that were serious. I first wanted to obtain my doctorate before I thought about marriage. He insisted that I keep the ring but I was not comfortable with that so I mailed the ring back to him at his home.

I attended New York University for two years, then took a year to prepare for my oral exams and another year to write my dissertation. I chose the topic of my dissertation carefully because I wanted it to be topical. I chose to write about the accounting practices of Public Utility companies in New York. It meant that I had to call on them and spend some time getting to know the people at Con Edison. As a result, I befriended some of the executives and was able to get all the information I needed.

Mindful of marriage

The first time I came to America I had promised my mother and my family that I would not marry an American. A Chinese woman could only marry a Chinese man. There was a double standard, though. A Chinese man could marry a Filipino woman but it was not acceptable for a Chinese woman to marry a Filipino man. Even worse was for a Chinese young lady to marry an American. This was family law.

The reasons were rooted in the Second World War. At that time, most of the American men in the Philippines were GIs and the girls who went out with them were considered to be loose. A young lady that came from a respectable family did not want to disgrace her family and so did not consort with American soldiers. (My sister, Hope, married a Filipino who was an American G.I.)

In my adult years in Manila, I had noted the way Chinese men treated their women and I much preferred the American way. So even while I was ambitiously pursuing my doctorate in economics, accounting and business, I had marriage half way on my mind.

It was towards the end of my fourth year that I started to think seriously about marriage. I had many dates. Yet I did not respond seriously to any of them. Now it was time to think about marriage and I put all the men I dated on a list. I also jotted down the pros and cons of each person so that I could better pick one. On one side of a piece of paper I wrote down the different characteristics like honesty, trustworthiness, religion, etc. Then on the top I wrote down the names of my different boyfriends. I also evaluated what they had to offer, how we would interact, and whether the marriage could be sustained for a long period.. Then I put points next to each category to weigh them and added the points.

I put Edward on my list even though I had no attraction to him and even though we had not dated much. Ed had always asked me to go to lectures while the other men in my life had asked me to nice places. I had told him that I spent all day in lectures and could see no reason why I would want to attend lectures at night as well. Ed and I did spend time together, though, for we went to Dr. von Mises' many suppers together and attended the same economics classes.

Ed scored the most points so I chose him. He was also the poorest financially. But as stated previously, money was not my priority

When I was a young girl, I used to pray that some day, if I ever got married, I would like to marry a poor man but a good and honest man for I had seen rich men in business and it was difficult for them to be faithful to one wife, especially after the wife aged. There was so much temptation with young, beautiful women who wanted money. I knew Edward was poor in material things but truly honest and that he would never lie to me.

After I married Ed, we were sometimes so hard-up that I used to say, "Boy, Ed, we are so poor."

Ed used to reply, "Isn't that what you prayed for? You got what you asked for!" I never regretted it.

Tom took it badly. He had a nervous breakdown and his parents committed him to an asylum. There he was given electric shock treatment and drugs that did not agree with him. He escaped and found his way to my apartment on Fifth Avenue. I was not happy to open the door to him. I had so many confused feelings: compassion, fear, guilt. I let him in because I could not leave him outside in the cold. I told him that I would let him in if he let me call his parents in New Jersey. He consented and after I called his parents, they came to fetch him.

Tom never married and I have often wondered about that. His sister and I still correspond and from time to time I hear about Tom. Many years later, in 1993, I received a letter from Tom via one of my students at Hillsdale College. I was an advisor to a freshman student from Maine. Tom had an aunt in Maine with a beautiful house where Ed and I spent a night in her Romeo and Juliet room on our honeymoon. After Tom's aunt died, he inherited the house. His next door neighbor told Tom that his son was going to Hillsdale College in Michigan and Tom knew I was teaching here, and thus, he wrote the letter. I cannot recall whether I replied to the letter; perhaps I did and perhaps I didn't. Tom's was one of those sad stories in my life.

Ed had an admirable background. He graduated from M.I.T with an engineering degree, then went to Boston College to obtain a Master's in Economics. After that, he obtained a Master's degree in philosophy from a Catholic university. Ed started a PhD (Economics) at Cornell University and then transferred to the University of Chicago. However, he was not happy with the perspectives and settled at New York University to complete his PhD under Dr. von Mises whom he admired.

Ed never spoiled me the way my other boyfriends did. On Mondays he always invited me to a lecture for the following Friday evening. I preferred to do more entertaining things and would tell him that I would let him know. If I received no other invitation, I would call him on Friday morning and he would travel a hundred blocks to fetch me.

As we attended the same classes and did the New York Times crossword puzzle together at coffee breaks, it was inevitable that we built a strong friendship.

After a year of this, he invited me to visit his brother in Tennessee and we drove there for Christmas. En route, we encountered a fierce snow storm and were forced to stop at the next motel. Ed went in to reserve a room with twin beds (we couldn't afford two rooms). The manager explained that he only had one room vacant and this had a queen sized bed. It was either that or wait the storm out in the car. So Ed took the room. A little while later, the manager came out to the car and said with a large smile on his face, "Are you the lady with the gentleman from New York?" I said yes and he escorted me inside.

I asked Ed what he had said to the man and Ed told me that he had told the man that he just wanted a room until the storm passed. The storm did not pass quickly and soon it became obvious that we would have to spend the night. So, I slept on one side of the bed under the blankets and Ed slept on the other side of the bed on top of the blankets.

Later, when we arrived at his brother Jack's house and told him the story, he said, "Don't tell that story to anyone. They won't believe you! But I believe you because I know my brother."

It was a good weekend and when we returned to New York, Ed and I were closer and I spent more time with him during the next year. In the meantime, my final exams were ahead, the work load was even heavier so I worked even harder.

Doctorate

My major required that I have a three hour oral exam conducted by six professors. Each professor would spend half an hour asking questions regarding his particular specialty. At the end of an hour and a half, there would be a fifteen minute break. During this time, the professors would decide if the student had shown sufficient knowledge and understanding to continue with the exam. If so, then they would request the student to return and the remaining three professors would question the student. At the end of the three hour ordeal they would confer and then call you in to tell you whether you had passed or failed. If you failed, you come back the next year and if you failed again, there would not be another opportunity to retake the exam. All the work would be for naught.

It was Professor von Mises who started the questioning. "Now, Miss Tan, there was a movement," he started, "it is a French word." Being nervous, I answered, "Sorry, Dr. von Mises, I don't speak French." I thought they would end the oral exam right there but my advisor turned to me, understanding that I had not understood the professor's accent and question.

"The professor means *laissez faire* economics," he informed me. My mind cleared. I shook off my nervousness and began to speak about the topics that I had been studying for the previous three years. I tried to read the professors' body language so that I could see if I was on the right track or not. Some had their faces glued to their newspapers while others appeared more user friendly.

At half time, I left the examination room and went to the bathroom, not sure whether I would be returning or not. Eventually, a professor came out and invited me to return for the second half. It was a happy moment. This time I was more confident. At the end of the session I was once more asked to leave the room while the professors conferred. This time, it was only five minutes before I was called in. They all looked at me with broad smiles. "Febes, the decision was unanimous. You made it!" I had passed the oral exam. Now all that remained was to write the dissertation for which I had set aside a year. I was elated!

As we all spoke, one of the professors took me aside and asked me how well I knew Dr. von Mises. I told him that I only knew Dr. von Mises as my lecturer and the occasional student supper at his home. I was then told that Dr. von Mises held me in high regard and had not stopped speaking about me for the entire time that they were evaluating my performance. He told them that I came from a very intelligent family although he knew nothing of my personal life.

In the years after I graduated from New York University (June, 1964), Ed and I were frequent visitors to Dr. von Mises and his wife, Margit. They were wonderful evenings and I learned something of his wife's background. She had been an actress in Austria but had not pursued her career in America. After Ed and I had children, we did not consider it good manners to have two young children causing havoc in the abode of two elderly people and so declined invitations more frequently. However, the von Mises' insisted on us bringing the kids whenever we were invited for a meal.

We last saw Dr. von Mises and his wife in late 1969. He passed away in October 1973. Dr. von Mises lives on for me and I treasure the knowledge he gave me. In turn, I have passed it on to my students and they, in turn, continue to pass it on to others. Since Hillsdale College believes in laissez faire principles, Dr. von Mises left most of his books and collections to Hillsdale College after he passed away. Mrs. Von Mises wrote a book and even mentioned Ed and me. She passed away in the late 80s.

Marriage plans

As the time approached for me to return home, Ed spoke to me of marriage. I had previously told him that if I returned to Manila, it was unlikely that I would return to New York. He, therefore, wanted me to marry him immediately, despite the fact that he had not yet finished his thesis. (Ed is very slow because he demands perfection.) I had been planning that after my graduation in June 1964, I would either return to Manila or marry so I accepted Ed's proposal.

We considered having the wedding ceremony in Manila but my mother and relatives would say that as we had traveled together we must already have slept together so there was no further point in marrying. They would then tell Ed to go back to the States. In the end I told Hope that I was getting married but never my mother or relatives in the Philippines. I knew that if I did, the family would forbid it. Marriage to an American man still wasn't acceptable.

The other plan was to marry in New York in July (a month after my graduation), and then take an around-the-world honeymoon with Manila as one of the stopovers. Because Ed was not well established financially, he couldn't afford a large wedding. So we planned to marry in the sacristy of a church - not at the main altar.

The wedding

Around this time I called my sponsor, Walter Ruthenburg, to tell him that I would not be returning to the Philippines as I was getting married. He was thrilled and wanted to know who the lucky groom was and what our wedding plans were. I told him the wedding would be simple because we were students and had little money. Uncle Walter, a Russian Jew, was not at all happy with this and approached a close friend who was a Monsignor. Monsignor offered to marry us in his church at St. Anne's, in Ossining, New York. I suggested that the Monsignor marry us in the Sacristy since neither Ed nor I had family in New York but both he and Uncle Walter insisted that I have the wedding that I dreamed of. No expense was to be spared!

This was typical of my sponsor. In the years that I had studied at New York University, he had called each week to hear of my progress. I would tell him that I had received As. "That's cause for a celebration!" he would say and I would either go to his office in Wall Street and we would have a meal close by, or we would party somewhere else.

July 5, 1964
St. Anne's Church,
Ossining, New York
Febes & Edward's
wedding

Eddie's baptism (1965) with Ed and Febes and Godparents, Jack Barlaam and Maria Petrucci.

Eddie Jr. and Betty in New York in 1967.

Eddie and Betty dressed for Halloween, 1969, in the Philippines

Eddie's birthday, New York, 1971, shortly before moving to Hillsdale

Now came a small difficulty. Father Paul, Ed's uncle, was a Jesuit priest, and he was accustomed to conducting the weddings and baptisms for his nephews and nieces. He wished to marry Ed and me. I played peacekeeper and said, "Father Paul, please don't get upset. The Monsignor offered to marry us and we've already accepted." We then reached a compromise and agreed that he would assist in the ceremony.

The wedding was to take place in the afternoon in Ossining, about two hour's travel from Manhattan. Father Paul would say Mass for us at St. Patrick's Cathedral in Manhattan on the morning of our wedding day and after that we would all drive to Ossining for the ceremony. So I was surprised to hear Father Paul tell Ed's brothers that the Mass would be at 10 a.m. I was about to correct him as Father Paul had told me earlier that the Mass was at 11 a.m. when I caught his eye. Some instinct made me remain silent and I did not say anything. A little while later I was told that Ed and his brothers had a susceptibility to being late and if I wanted them to be on time, I had to allow for that lateness. True to form, on the morning of the Mass, Hope and I were already in church when Ed, along with his brothers, Jerry and Jack, walked in at 10.30. Instead of being half an hour late, they were now half an hour early!

Our simple wedding turned out to be a rather grand affair at the big church in Ossining. A white carpet was laid from the door to the altar and there were matching flowers and garlands at each pew. It was an elegant contrast to the Monsignor's royal red robes. When Uncle Walter gave me away (for that was his only request since he never had a daughter), it seemed to me that I was truly blessed with wonderful people in my life.

The reception was held at the Tappan Zee Restaurant, near Tappan Zee Bridge in New York. We had dinner, music and dancing for about fifty guests. These were mutual friends from the university, as well as Hope and Ed's relatives (some of whom traveled some distance to attend).

After the reception, we drove away in the Monsignor's black Cadillac (decorated with white flowers) to the Motel on the Mountain in Suffern, New York. Later, I heard a story that the Monsignor and some friends were going to play a trick on Ed and me by sending a policeman to knock on our door and ask us for our marriage license. In those days, it was not permitted for unmarried couples to stay in the same hotel room and it took a few weeks to process the marriage license. They decided, however, that it would scare us so they didn't go ahead with the prank.

Ed and I had planned a honeymoon trip around the world and had paid for the trip and received our immunization shots but it was not to be. When I went to Immigration, I was told that my status would change on the day I married an American citizen. I would no longer be classified as a Filipino student. Subsequently, I wouldn't be permitted to re-enter the country. "If you leave, you won't be able to come back as a student as you are the wife of an American and you will have to wait about ten years in the Philippines in order to get a visa," one official told me. We therefore spent our honeymoon settling into our new two bedroom apartment which was within walking distance of St. John's University, in Queens, New York.

Professor!

Two months after my marriage I started teaching at St. John's University while Ed stayed at home so that he could finish his dissertation. I was terrified of standing in front of the class and told Ed. "Just try," he said "and if you can't do it, you can quit!." So I tried it.

I have never forgotten my first day of teaching at St. John's. So nervous was I that I had prepared twenty pages of notes in case I became tongue-tied. My heart was pounding loudly and I was sure everybody else could hear it as I walked to the door of my class. The students sitting at their desks were a blur to me as I approached the podium.

The class hadn't started yet and there were more students coming so I busied myself with my notes while I waited. I was aware that I spoke English with an accent, that I was an Oriental woman teaching U.S. income tax, something that was highly unusual. I was also aware that they were mostly male students and that they were accustomed to being taught by American men. I was about to break the mold – again.

Then a student arrived. He looked at me and then at the class. It was obvious he recognized some of his classmates. He turned to me and said, "Are you the professor that is teaching us?"

His demeanor told me plainly that this was not what he wished or anticipated. He clearly felt unable to respect the input of an Oriental woman. When I nodded, he looked at me for a moment and walked out.

The rest of the class watched my reaction. I was impassive and continued to study my notes. More students arrived. Then the student who had scurried off to the administrative office to voice a complaint about my status, returned. It seemed that he had been given no other option. He made his way to the back of the classroom and faced me with a sneering attitude. I ignored it.

It was time to commence class - time to pray, as was the custom at this Catholic university.

"Please stand for prayer," I said to my students. Some stood while others did not. I waited, then repeated myself. "As a courtesy to those around you," I continued, "please stand." Begrudgingly, the remainder of the students stood. "Father," I prayed, "please guide us today as we seek your Almighty strength and wisdom." In my heart I prayed that the Lord would guide me.

Then it was time to start. I had prepared my speech.

"If you have any comments or criticism, you should express yourselves with the intention that it will be constructive criticism. I cannot change my accent but if I talk too fast, please let me know. Cheating will not be tolerated and I will show no mercy if you do, so don't even think about it. However, if you have a problem you can come to me and I will always be available to listen and will try to help."

At times, my voice sunk to a whisper and I had to remind myself to be confident. After all, I told myself, I am the boss and know better than any of them! I had to give myself confidence and remind myself that I had been to Stanford and had been one of two women among two hundred men. I had also obtained my PhD at New York University. I chanted these things to myself as one chants a mantra. Those thoughts gave me the confidence to continue. It was enough. I did not even look at my notes.

Over the next week, I gained confidence rapidly. I made a point of knowing all my students in class and soon they developed confidence in me. This spurred me on and I was looking forward to adding more subjects to my curriculum when I discovered that I was pregnant.

I was to give birth the following April - exactly nine months after my marriage to Ed. The year was 1964 and I was thirty six years old. I was thrilled that I was going be a mother.

Perhaps, though, because it was mostly a male class, I was a bit embarrassed at being pregnant in front of my students and, soon, they noticed my condition. One time, an older male student came up from the back row of the classroom and whispered something to me. He told me the price tag of my new maternity dress was in full view of the class. I smiled as I removed it and turned to the class. They had a good laugh and I realized that they were comfortable with me.

I taught for one semester as the baby would be born before the second semester ended and it was easier for the university to find a professor to teach a full semester than for half a semester.

I was not covered by the school's health insurance and could not take paid maternity leave because I had only been teaching for one semester. Ed and I survived because we both had a habit of skimping. Ed's habit was no doubt caused by being an orphan with little money while the war years had made it a life long practice for me to look at every penny twice before spending it. We saved whatever we could. We had set aside money for the hospital and for the doctor's bills. We even had enough to buy a washing machine and dryer.

A miracle baby

On the day that Eddie was to be born, Father Paul and Ed's younger brother, Jerry, were staying with us overnight in New York. I started having labor pains early in the morning but still prepared breakfast, lunch and dinner for them. All three of them went to St. John's University to celebrate Mass with Father Paul. When they got back, Ed took me to the hospital and left me there because the nurse said that the baby wasn't due yet. I sent him home to take care of our guests.

Within a few hours, Eddie was born. It was Palm Sunday, 11 April, 1965. Happily, the delivery was normal and I only stayed the obligatory three days in the hospital. Then we returned home to our apartment in Queens, New York.

Eddie cried a lot. He slept little and it became obvious that he was suffering from something that he found painful. I wasn't feeling wonderful either. I consulted the pediatrician and he told me to bring my baby to his office right away. After examining him, he found that Eddie's navel was infected where the cord had been cut. It looked as if the surgical instrument hadn't been sufficiently sterilized . As Eddie had been circumcised with the same instrument, there was a dual infection

Eddie's temperature had risen to 102° and the doctor told me not to wait but to take our little baby back to hospital in Manhattan immediately. Both Ed and I were crying in the car on the way to the hospital. Once Ed and I arrived, a team of doctors took Eddie from my arms and examined him. They shook their heads and my heart started playing leapfrog as I felt bolts of anxiety shoot through me. My fears were not unwarranted.

"There is a fifty-fifty chance that we can save him," the doctor informed us after examining him. I couldn't bear to lose my baby. I was tired from being kept up throughout the night by the cries of my baby and I had been infected from the same knife when the cord was cut. It was one of the lowest points of my life but even here, my faith held me up. I battled on, praying, hoping.

Eddie was placed in an isolation ward on the top floor of the hospital. I stayed with my new born baby from six in the morning to midnight each day. Then I would take the subway back to Queens at midnight and return early the next morning to breastfeed him. Sometimes, when I arrived at Eddie's room, he had cried himself out. He had no more voice and sorrow and pain were etched deeply in his eyes. His tiny, naked body was covered with a dried scale every morning. My body ached. My mind was numb. Both of us were growing weaker by the hour and after a week of this, I thought that I could not continue anymore. I could not bring myself to eat and prayer became my sustenance.

While walking on the streets of Manhattan, from the subway to the hospital, I thought I was going to collapse in the street. It occurred to me that nobody would know who I was. What would happen to my baby? At the end of nine long days, a doctor came into the isolation ward and told me that little Eddie was well and that I could take him home the next day. I was too tired to feel elated but gratitude towards God flowed through me.

Ever practical, I went to the office to ask what the bill would be. I was told that it would be a thousand dollars. One thousand dollars was a lot of money in those days. The doctor left the room and I stood staring down at my baby son whose life had been granted to me through my endless prayer. If prayer could save the life of my child, I thought, could it not bring me the money by the following morning? There was nothing left for it but to pray - although there were moments when I did not know how to do that anymore.

Miracle provision
There was a knock at the door and I thought, "What now?"
"Come in," I said, my voice a bare whisper.

At the door stood a former business associate from the Philippines, Ben Lee. He was in New York on business and had called our home. Ed had told him where I was as well as given him the details of the situation. Ben asked me how I was, then asked me to give him my hand. He put something in my hand. Then he left without even entering the room. It seemed he had to catch a plane. He told me that after he had spoken to Ed, he had called my former boss, Johnny. Johnny hadn't spoken to me for a year because he was upset that I had married. Nevertheless, he told Ben to call on me and to give the baby a gift. When I went back inside the room, I opened my hand and counted ten one hundred dollar bills. I couldn't believe it. I said, "Lord, if I had found this money in the street, I would have returned it to the police because it would not have been mine. But Thou hast found a way to help us. Thank you, my dearest Lord, for when I am all the way down, you come and pick me up."

Once more, there had been an element of miraculous timing to my prayer. There had been an orchestration of events that I had come to know and trust. That serendipity was to become a staple in my life and I have always believed that this is the way that God answers prayers – by synchronizing events to give us the very best for our lives.

The next day when I left the hospital, I was able to pay the bill in full.

Pearls of wisdom

Many years ago, I started writing down notes that came about as a result of my prayer time. To date, I have 128 of these little note books. As I started to look back on my life, I began to reread these. In doing so, I remembered lessons and had realizations that I had long forgotten but that had woven themselves into the fabric of my life. Even though I wasn't consciously aware of them, they were there, silently making a difference.

Each person's life is like a book with each page representing a day. Sometimes a page has many gems and sometimes it lacks any real merit or content. Like reading a thriller, we often want to know the outcome upfront. Simultaneously, we do not want the story to end. However, all stories come to an end: some end sadly, others end happily, and others end in ways we do not know. On our last day here, our story is ended, and God decides whether it was a book worth reading or a book without merit.

Sometimes I visualize this world a hundred years ago. How many people from that time are alive now? Only a few. Life is short. Eternity is not. How can we describe or fathom eternity? The most we will live to be is one hundred years or so - that is a one with two zeroes. Eternity is another matter; if we filled this entire world with zeroes and put them next to the number one, we would not have even come close to the end of eternity. There is no end to eternity.

According to Catholicism, God gave us free will and sent us the Ten Commandments. If we choose not to follow those Commandments, He will send us to the eternal fires of hell. We are free to choose whichever path we wish. Wisdom is understanding how our choices bring about the situations we find ourselves in.

Interestingly, many people nowadays prefer to find a scapegoat rather than take personal responsibility for the outcome of their choices. One cannot pull the wool over God's eyes, though, for He is all-seeing. Nor can one sue him. We have the option of asking for forgiveness and because He loves us, He will always do so.

The problem with playing the blame game is that He cannot forgive us for something for which we say we are not responsible. (There's nothing to forgive.) There are many advantages to admitting our errors. One advantage is that we are able to learn from our mistakes once we are able to examine them. We then make better decisions for our lives and better outcomes follow. Another advantage is that we no longer carry the unconscious baggage that hinders us in our day to day lives. Forgivenesss from God clears us of the heavy mantle that sin casts over us.

Marriage to Ed

Through the years of my marriage to Ed, there have been the normal ups and downs that every marriage has. For us the differences have been intellectual arguments rather than differences in values. We both believe that marriage is for life, for better or worse. This is in accordance with our Catholic beliefs. We have never gone to bed angry with each other and the fact that we could communicate easily, has kept us close.

We made a promise on our wedding day, when we looked at each other with eyes full of love, that we would never go to bed angry. I never imagined that it would be difficult for me to keep that promise for I had quite a temper at that time. There were times when it would be near midnight and we would be in bed - back to back. Ed would turn around and hug me and say, "I'm sorry." That touched me and taught me a lesson because it was usually my fault and not Ed's. It helped me to realize that I was not perfect and that I needed to learn to apologize. So without too many spoken words, Ed's example taught me to be humble.

Ed is six feet tall and weighed 180 lbs when we got married. I fed him steak, pizza and other delicious food and by the end of the first year, his weight had soared to 210 lbs. One St. Patrick's Day, I surprised him with an Irish dinner of corned beef and cabbage. Because the only corned beef I knew was the canned variety, I used that and sautéed it with thinly sliced cabbage. When he came home from school, he saw the dish on the table and asked me what it was. I replied, "Corned beef and cabbage." I thought he would appreciate my cooking but he said, "You silly dilly – Irish corned beef, cabbage and potatoes are cut in chunks and boiled." But he ate it anyway.

About midnight, I found him doubled over on the bathroom floor. He was having excruciating stomach pains so I called our landlord from downstairs and he took us to the hospital while his wife watched our kids. On examining Ed, the doctor said that his appendix had burst and he would need surgery in the morning. So I went home with the landlord and left Ed at the hospital. Early the next morning, the surgeon gave me a ride to the hospital. I sat in the waiting room and when the surgery was over, the nurse wheeled Ed to a room that he would share with another patient. I looked at Ed as he was taken to the ward. He was still under anesthesia and was as pale as the bed sheets that covered him. I walked next to the bed while it was being wheeled and whispered in Ed's ear, that if he got well, I would not nag him anymore. After the nurse left, Ed sat up and started pulling out the IVs. His eyes were glazed so I knew that he did not know what he was doing. I yelled for help and some nurses came at once. They put Ed in a straight jacket and gave him another shot. Later, they told me that had Ed remained in the recovery room, there would have been nobody to notice that he had pulled the IV out. Since it had been an emergency surgery, the recovery room had been fully booked and Ed had had to transfer to another ward. When a patient wakes up from anesthesia, he has the same frame of mind that he had when he went under. Ed had woken up fighting because that had been his reaction when he went under. Had I not been there, Ed might have died.

The surgeon said that Ed had been lucky as there was a kink in his appendix and this had slowed down the flow of the poison. Later on, after Ed recovered, he told me that a Chinese leprechaun played a trick on him - eating the corned beef and cabbage Chinese style. The incident traumatized Ed to some extent and he developed an interest in finding a healthier lifestyle.

When Ed and I moved with the kids to Manila in 1967 to help Johnny with his business (we took a leave of absence from St. John's University), Ed had plenty of free time. In New York he had to teach and help me take care of the kids. In Manila all he had to do was finish his dissertation. So, he would come to the office with me each day, not as an employee of the company, but to be with me while he wrote his dissertation. After work, we would go to the mall and I would get my exercise, sauna and massage. He would go to the book store and browse. While there, he became interested in vegetarianism and nature cure and bought and read many books about the subject. The first Thanksgiving that we were in Manila, the table was set with a big turkey and all the trimmings for dinner. Quite unexpectedly, Ed announced that he was not going to eat meat anymore and that day was the start of a new lifestyle for him.

After Ed became a vegetarian, he lost a lot of weight. He also did not need his eyeglasses anymore and never wore them again. He wore glasses for the first few years of our marriage and, after he became a vegetarian, never needed them again. He attributed it to his diet.

My husband is conservative in many areas. For example, he believes that women should always wear skirts and he will not open the car door for me if I'm wearing pants. He doesn't like me to wear make-up and he likes me to cover my head. I laugh at him and tell him that he wouldn't recognize me if I dressed like that. Independence of mind is something that both Ed and I share.

Our children, too, have an innate independence of mind. Sometimes, it made for clashing times in our home. I found myself intervening for them with my husband, convincing him that they were children growing up, involved in a current fad and that it would pass.

Ed does not understand loving in the same way that others do although we love each other dearly. He does not know how to give unconditionally and so whenever he does give something, there are strings attached. Perhaps this is why he feels the need to bribe people to do something. For instance, when he wanted Eddie and Betty to read books on Catholicism, he slipped ten dollar bills in every few pages.

When Eddie and Betty were in their early thirties, I sat down one day to speak to them about these altercations. "He didn't grow up in an atmosphere of love and he doesn't know how to express it. By this time, you must make allowances for him and not be so intolerant of him."

Things have been better since then and they respect him now for who he is: He is a man that when he is determined to do something, will do it, despite all opposition. They know that he is honest and loves them in his own way.

Ed reads a lot about the government and about different groups like Jews, the media, Hollywood and how newspapers are sometimes controlled by these groups. He also blames his uncle, Father Paul, for not converting his mother from Christian Science to Catholicism before she died. The Church has meant much to both of us in our lives.

Perhaps, the one thing that brings me sorrow is that Ed no longer attends church with me. Ed says his Mass prayers in Latin on Sundays and holy days of obligation. We even have a solarium in our house where he prays. Ed doesn't believe that the present church is the church of his youth. He says that there have been too many changes so he now avoids the church. We used to go to Mass every day before we were married but not anymore.

I know that this is a matter of conscience and I respect it. We are all answerable to God for our actions and I cannot judge another for I do not know and cannot read the inner workings of a heart and mind. Ed understands this for he has an open heart.

The crosses that I carry in my marriage are not many. They are his eating habits and religion. However, we have an undying love for each other and this keeps us focused on what is important.

Now, in our retirement, we each continue as we did before. We each have our own interests. Ed is a true intellectual and reads and writes all day long. I do not know the details but that is okay with me. I meet with friends, am actively involved with the Church, and occasionally become involved in a project. My current project involves getting my life story down on paper so that there is some record of my life and that of my family, both past and present. I feel that my life has been unique as I have lived in a time and a place that bridged the eastern world of the 19th century with the western world of the 21st century. I would like my children to have something to tell their children and I would also like to leave a record of the way life used to be. Also, if through writing down some of the wisdom that I have gained, it encourages or teaches someone something, then it has been a worthwhile project.

But back to the early days of our marriage, to the time Eddie was a small boy, and Betty had just been born. Somewhere within the two month period of my honeymoon, I had applied to become an American citizen and, three years later, I had taken the oath and become an American citizen.

Marino & Joe

The year, 1967, was not a good year. In April, my brother, Marino, died in Manila. He had not been feeling well and Estela, his wife, took him to the hospital. The next morning he passed on leaving Estela to raise twelve children on her own. Nine days later, Joe, Hope's husband died at home in Vancouver, Washington. Joe had been feeling fine. They were both lying in bed and Hope heard Joe inhale air but could not hear any air coming out. She called her daughter, Marie, who called the emergency department of the hospital. When Joe arrived at the hospital, he was no longer alive.

Hope was devastated and sunk into a deep depression. Joe Jr. was away from home at that time, and in his second year at West Point Military Academy. Marie was seventeen, a junior at high school and living at home.

She needed to do something so in September she rented out her house, moved to Seattle, Washington and started College. Dorm life was fun for her. She didn't have to cook or put aside her own needs in order to provide for someone else. She had the freedom to do what she wanted when she wanted, and in time, she recovered from her depression.

Initially, she signed up for economics but the person teaching wasn't a professor and she found it difficult to understand what he was saying. So she switched majors – this time to languages. After she completed her major (Spanish), she stayed another year in order to earn a certificate to teach.

After Hope returned to Vancouver, she taught Spanish for two years at Junior College. By that time, the grief caused by Joe's death, had subsided, though she never stopped missing him.

Manila

About a month after I received my American citizenship in 1967, Johnny called from the Philippines and explained that one of his top executives had died and he needed me. It was three in the morning and I was not *compos mentis*. Later, I asked Ed what I had said. "That you would accept the position," Ed told me.

I had been teaching for three years by that time. Little Eddie was three years old and Betty a year and a half. Ed and I discussed it. He was still working on his dissertation so it seemed a good way to meet all our needs. He would not be working in Manila and therefore would be able to complete his dissertation. I would be the breadwinner as Johnny would compensate me the equivalent of both our salaries and there would be servants to look after the children. Plus, of course, the money would buy far more in Manila than it did in America.

Ironically, my status had changed and I was now an American citizen and could not work in the Philippines. I had to call Johnny back and explain this to him. Johnny soon resolved the situation by arranging with an American cigarette company that he imported raw materials from to hire me as a consultant. Soon we were winging our way to Manila.

The perks included a mansion, a car, five servants, a driver, and a gardener. I had carpenters make our furniture and purchased all the soft furnishings for our new home. Eddie and Betty each had their own amah (nurse) and my mother, Susie, came to live with us. I was glad to have her nearby. We had a close relationship.

I drifted back to my former life with ease, managing Johnny's extensive business interests and, at times, working long hours to get the work done. Each morning, there would be reports from the many companies on my desk. Sometimes, I would visit these companies because there were newer and better methods that could be used and so I journeyed to Hong Kong, Taipei, Borneo and Japan. I would meet with the presidents of the companies and negotiate contracts. In the evening, they would take me out to dinner.

The work was varied. Johnny had an extensive business portfolio, owning amongst others, the President Hotel in Taipei (at the time the best accommodation available), a bank in Hong Kong, two steel plants, a plywood company, and the distributorship for American cigarettes. In Borneo, Johnny's company not only owned the rubber plantation, but the island on which the plantation was situated. All the people living on the island were part of the company.

In my work, I would meet with presidents and chairmen of companies, with tax representatives and other luminaries. I would also attend prestigious functions at places like Malacanang Palace, the residence of Ferdinand and Imelda Marcos. I loved the clothes, the glamour, the important people.

The décor and architecture was impressive and the catering was sometimes too lavish to describe. I wished I could have shared some of these delicacies with Ed but with his new vegetarian way of life, Ed would not consider eating the many different foods that I did. In fact, getting Ed to eat was quite a problem.

As a result of his new vegetarian regime, Ed lost quite a bit of weight within a few months and my mother and I became seriously concerned. "Look at him. He's so thin," my mother would say and Ed would reply, "Look at her. She's got heart trouble and eats meat."

Eventually, I started nagging Ed to see a doctor for a check up. Ed's response was, "I love you." This was our personal code for 'No'. Things became tense between us and I moved into a hotel because the rift between us had widened considerably. I'd like to say that Ed saw sense when he saw that he was going to lose me but that was not what happened.

Instead, a friend talked him into going for a medical check up. Ed selected a vegetarian doctor (at a Seventh Day Adventist hospital), believing that he would be vindicated in his eating habits. He was to find out from the American doctor that he was malnourished as well as undernourished and that he needed to eat properly. Indeed, the doctor informed him that, far from improving his health, he was endangering it. The doctor suggested peanut butter and unrefined bread which contained gluten (grain protein). Together, these would provide the essential protein that his body needed.

Cultural perspectives

There were many small incidents during our time there. Earlier in my life, I would have accepted these incidents as perfectly normal. After my exposure to the west, they seemed to me to be rather bizarre.

Servants were part of the family and their problems were our problems. We fed them, we housed them, we took an interest in their ups and downs; yet we were always aware that there was a culture of stealing.

Those who are unaccustomed to living in these areas often do not comprehend the intricacies of the relationship. They are shocked at arbitrary statements like, 'servants take what isn't theirs'. Small pieces of soap left on a basin might disappear and a new bar of soap opened earlier than might have been necessary. The last inch of dishwashing liquid might vanish before the household had its full use of it. Or, perhaps, money not kept under lock and key would disappear.

I recall one particular incident. Something I had valued had gone missing. I asked the servant what had happened to it. "I don't know," she replied, "perhaps, the elves took it." It was difficult to know what to reply to this. Did I debate the non-existence of elves and demand a more rational explanation? Did I ask the servant to leave my employ? Did I call the police? Or did I simply accept that I would get no further and accept my loss?

Servants are an integral part of life in the Philippines. There is no middle class; one percent is rich and the other ninety-nine percent are poor. If the poor are not employed as servants, then there would be even less work as industry is not sufficiently developed to provide jobs for all. Accordingly, servants have a tremendous fear of losing their positions as this is often the only way they have of sustaining themselves and their families. Whatever salary they get is net income.

In the end, I kept the servant. It was the only humane thing to do.

Motherhood

Life might have continued in Manila in this manner indefinitely as it was pleasant and I was deeply committed to my work. Then there occurred an incident that gave me another perspective of how things were in my life.

One day, when Eddie was about five years old, we were all gathered in the garden and Eddie fell down and skinned his knee. He jumped up and ran to his amah for comfort. I called him and hugged him. "What does Mommy do for you?" I asked.

Eddie looked at me with his large eyes full of tears and said, "Let me think. Mommy brings me toys."

"What else does Mommy do?" I asked him, waiting with a mother's heart for his sweet reply.

"That's all," he said.

I was stunned. My child did not know who I was. My child was closer to his amah than to me. I was deeply hurt and realized that my children's childhood days were short and I couldn't buy them back once they had become adults. The affection and respect of children towards parents is gained when they are young. If I was not home often enough to form that bond, then what good would it do me to have a million dollars in the bank and a glamorous career?

That was the end of my career as a consultant. I went to Johnny the next day and tendered my resignation. It was a sad parting and although I saw Johnny from time to time when I traveled to Manila in future years, we were never that close again. He died in 1992 but the friendship I established with both his wives and his family lives on. I still receive Christmas cards from his head wife.

Ed and I returned to New York where we resumed our teaching positions at St. Johns University.

Pearl of wisdom

I think that in many ways I've been a step ahead of most women. Firstly, I went to Stanford University to get my MBA when there were not many women going after that degree. Then, I went on to consulting work and, again, there were not many women in that profession.

After I married and had kids, I shelved consulting work and went into the teaching profession so I could be home with our children. This was in direct contravention of the growing women's lib movement at that time. I was lucky that my husband was also a professor and that our schedule allowed us to arrange our time so that one of us was always home. We both understood the importance and obligations of parenthood, and accepted less work rather than send our kids to a daycare center.

Nowadays, there are more women in business and they try to juggle jobs and motherhood. They take their kids to daycare centers. When they get home, they are tired but want to give their kids, 'quality time'. I never understood the concept of quality time. Do they think that spoiling their kids for an hour or two will compensate for the job they didn't do?

No daycare center can provide the one-on-one attention that each child needs in order to gain the emotional security, the language skills, and the social development that only twenty-four-hour-a-day parenthood supplies.

Children need their mothers to be there to kiss their hurts away when they fall down, to feed them nutritional foods for good development, and to give them the required information when they need it, not ten years later when problems arise.

I think that there are a growing number of women who are realizing that success in business is not all that it is made out to be, so they are quitting their high paying jobs to take care of their children. The years of childrearing are short and it is not possible to revisit them in order to rectify the things that were left undone. Too many parents today wonder why it is that when they gave their children material things during their growing years, the children are not there to return the favor in their declining years. The truth of the matter is that children need religious and moral training and the best training is by constant example. There is also the matter that close bonds cannot be formed with a parent unless there is initial 24 hour a day contact. In later life, if bonds aren't as strong as parents would wish them to be, they might look back to see how much time they spent with their children in their developing years.

Money in the bank can never compensate for a bond that was not developed in early years. Nor can it compensate for young lives that were never adequately developed through a deficiency of attention in their early years.

I was lucky to have learned my lesson early. There was a moment of insight and in that moment I made a decision that my children came first. So I decided to forego the lure of money, status and glamour and to continue as a college professor. As it turned out, Ed and I were doubly blessed in that we taught both our kids in college.

School life

Upon our return to New York in 1970, we settled in Henley Road in Queens. Ed and I went back to our previous teaching positions at St. John's University and Eddie and Betty went to a private school - Croydon Country Day School. Betty was four years old and she was already taking French and writing book reports with footnotes, bibliography and table of contents.

Ed and I, strongly aware of our responsibilities as parents, arranged our schedule so that there was always someone at home with the children. In addition, New York had a lot to offer and we took Betty and Eddie to museums, to parks and to other attractions.

I also had a part time position at Columbia Graduate School of Business and taught accounting there. After my job at St. John's University was done, I would go home and make dinner for Ed and the kids. My life was very busy with a full teaching load at St. John's University, a part time professorship at Columbia Graduate School of Business, and the tasks of mother and wife.

There were incidents that characterized my teaching style. One day, in the early 70s, when the draft for Vietnam was in full swing, a young man came to me and said, "Dr. Facey, if I don't do well in this course, I will be shipped to Vietnam," insinuating that if he got killed, I was responsible. I said to him, "You have to work for your grades." I was quite clear to my students that their marks were earned, their efforts rewarded, and that there were no short cuts.

Home life

There were incidents at home as well.

One day Betty had an ear infection. I took her to the doctor and the doctor wanted to operate to put tubes in her ear. I was alarmed and Ed insisted we take her to a Nature Cure doctor. The doctor said we should fast her for a week. I didn't want to do that either. We went to another medical doctor and he prescribed some medicine which I bought. Ed didn't want me to give her the medicine. He wanted me to fast her. She was only four years old.

After a day's fasting, Betty came to the kitchen where I was making dinner, begging for food. She asked me for something to eat so I gave her a small plate of spaghetti. At that moment, Ed came into the kitchen and saw the plate of spaghetti. He told me that Betty could not have it. Angry, I went to the bedroom, collected my purse and ran downstairs and got into the car. He followed me and climbed into the passenger side of the car. I told him to get out but he said he would go with me wherever I went. It was a good thing that Hope was visiting us at the time otherwise the children would have been left on their own. I went to the church in Queens. It was about 7 p.m. when I knocked at the door of the rectory and asked to see a priest.

The priest took us to a room and, amidst tears, I told him all the things that had happened since Ed and I married. I must have talked for over an hour without interruption, although I did tell Ed to butt in if I said anything that was not true. The priest listened patiently and then said to Ed, "Ed, I do not know much about vegetarianism or the nature cure. Therefore, if I have to make a decision, I will favor your wife because I have the same belief as your wife. Ask yourself, 'What is my priority in life? My vegetarianism and nature cure – or my family?' If this is your priority, you will lose your wife and children."

Ed said, "My priority is my wife and children."

So the priest told us to go home and make a compromise. Ed came up with a compromise. He would prepare a salad for dinner three nights a week and I would make more conventional dishes four nights a week.

Hope comes to visit

In 1972, Hope came to stay with us in New York. She loved it and decided to travel to China that same year, a year in which only a handful of people visited there. Nixon was one of them. That started her travel bug and, for a while, Hope traveled extensively. Finally, in 1976, she returned permanently to Vancouver, where she still lives.

There she joined the American Association of University Women. The organization attempts to get young women to select science and math for their majors. It also, however, provided many other services, for example, book clubs, and each month, Hope would read a book and and then meet with the group to discuss it. As a result, even though she never traveled as intensively again, her mind continued to broaden.

A change of tenure

Ed was always interested in free-market economics and had a close friend who was a member of the Foundation for Economic Education in New York. As a result of this friendship, Ed received an invitation to a dinner party and met Dr. George Roche, President of Hillsdale College in Hillsdale, Michigan.

Hillsdale was a 150 year old private college facing financial difficulty at the time. The College focused on liberal arts with a small economics faculty. My husband and the Hillsdale College president talked and soon Ed had an offer of employment. It was everything that he dreamed of. Ed was also not happy to bring up the children in New York and wanted a more countrified environment.

Ed was insistent that Hillsdale College find something for me to teach as he made it clear that he could not accept the position if there was nothing for me. So I found myself an Associate Professor teaching finance, marketing, and investments at a college that did not have an accounting department. The contract was for one year only and it would ensure that we both lose our tenure at St. John's University. The staff at St. John's were shocked and the Dean offered to keep our positions open for a year in case things did not work out for us at Hillsdale. While I was deeply touched at this offer, I could not accept it in good conscience and said so. Nevertheless our positions were kept open for three years. Every Christmas break, St. John's University would call me and ask if we were ready to return. (In all I taught at St. John's for seven years, having taken a sabbatical leave for two years to do consulting work in the Philippines.

In order to accept the position at Hillsdale College, not only would Ed have to take a substantial pay cut but the children and I, who loved New York, would be uprooted from an environment we loved.

Hillsdale had a population of about 7,500 in 1973 and the college had about 1000 fee paying students. In the summer, when the students were on vacation, Hillsdale county would lose about 10% of its population.

I did not want to move. The children did not want to move. But Ed did. As I was a good Chinese wife wanting to make her husband happy, we moved to Hillsdale. The year was 1973 and my family and I were beginning a new life.

Hillsdale

My first impression of Hillsdale was that it was a little town and that it could not possibly compare with New York. Still, it was my husband's wish and therefore I had to make the best of it. We decided on a country house and bought our first house about five miles outside the town on five acres of land.

Tenure

Ed and I started teaching at Hillsdale but while Ed was delighted at his position, I longed to teach accounting. From time to time, I would broach opening an accounting major but it was not something a college well known for its liberal arts program wanted to consider. There was another reason as well: The school did not have the funds to hire another professor. Eventually, at a faculty meeting, I offered to add one or two accounting courses every semester and to teach them gratis. This would be in addition to my other classes, so whereas the normal schedule would involve some twelve teaching hours, my new schedule would vary between eighteen and twenty one hours.

As it was not possible to offer all the courses necessary during Spring and Fall, I taught certain courses each summer. Generally summer courses were not well attended but the accounting courses were different as they could only be taken in the summer.

I was working around the clock now. I was up at 5.30 each morning. I would then prepare breakfast and lunches for Ed and the children, feed the dog, and tidy what needed to be tidied. At 7 a.m. I would depart for school so I could be ready for my 7.50 am class. I would remain at the school all day and if I was not teaching I would be in my office, available to students that needed further assistance. In the meantime, the children would be given a ride to the college and spent the rest of the day there, waiting for Ed and I to drive home. We left late afternoon at about 5 p.m. Then it was a five mile drive home and when I arrived, I would prepare dinner. This was not a simple matter as our children wanted American food like spaghetti, Ed wanted vegetarian food and I wanted Chinese. So for dinner, I usually made three different dishes.

As the children didn't have me all day, I would spend the next three or four hours with them. They would be in bed by 9 p.m. and then I would begin to grade student papers, prepare lectures and exams. This would take me up to 1 a.m. when I would finally put my head to pillow and sleep deeply.

In Search of the Pearl of Great Price

In 1997, I received a letter from Stanford University's Graduate School of Business (GSB) reminding me that our 40th alumni reunion was coming up. They sent me a list of my former classmates and their titles, e.g. CEOs, admirals, investment bankers, professors, etc. It was quite an impressive list of who's who. There was also a note asking each alumnus to write something for the memory book they are putting together. Of course, there was an invitation to attend all the ceremonies and make a contribution as well.

At the time I received the invitation, I was planning a trip to the Middle East with my husband. That trip would have included the reunion date, so I told the planning committee I would not be able to make it. The trip was canceled and I ended up missing both events. However, I still wished to share my thoughts and some stories of the years of yore with my friends, so I wrote a paragraph or two about the 'Search for the Pearl of Great Price' for the memory book.

It was published on the Stanford website for about a year.

God's call

Since there was not much entertainment in this small town, I decided to go back to reading the Bible as I had not opened it for many years. I opened the Bible and read the selection where it had opened. The next night I did the same thing and the Bible opened to the same chapter. I read it again. The third night I closed my eyes and asked the Lord to lead me and I opened the Bible once more to the same page. I was getting upset with God and I said, "Lord, what is your message? I have not read the Bible for many years and now that I want to go back to reading it, I keep opening to the same page – three times in a row." When I looked at the page, the only sentence I could read was, "Could you not watch one hour with me?" It was the question that Jesus asked his disciples when they were in the Garden of Gethsemane and He found them sleeping upon his return from prayer.

My hair stood on end.

I said, "Lord I do not have much time to sleep but I will start with six minutes," but it did not work. I would set the alarm for 4.30 am and when it went off, I would turn it off and ask the Lord for another minute of sleep. But that minute would be an hour so I lost my time with Him again. Then I asked Ed to push me out of bed when the alarm went off but it didn't work because the alarm didn't wake him. Next, I asked the Lord for help. He provided it in the form of one of those serendipitous events. From that time on, at about 4.30 each morning, I would hear a bird calling so loudly that I felt as if it was in my ear, "Phoebe, Phoebe, Phoebe."

I would say, "Okay, okay, I'm up," and so with the help of the bird, I was able to get up at 4.30 am. When I became used to this routine, I never heard the bird again.

Once when I was visiting Hope, I told her the story about the Phoebe bird. I said that I must be going crazy. She is member of the Audobon Society and she showed me a picture of a Phoebe bird in her bird book. This was one of my many experiences where God used his awesome power of synchronicity, through timing and proximity, to answer my prayer.

Carmelo

In 1980, Ed and I were asked to host an exchange student. His name was Carmelo and he was from Spain. He was a little older than Eddie and Betty but when Ed discovered that Carmelo was both vegetarian and Catholic, he agreed to let him live with us. After he moved in with us, we found out that Carmelo had listed that he was a vegetarian on his application but that his mother was not in agreement with this and had made him promise that he would eat meat in the United States.

I prepared breakfast and lunch boxes for Betty and Eddie and gave Carmelo some money to buy his lunch at school as he was not happy with the food we provided. Ed and I had made a compromise some years earlier that for three nights a week he would prepare salads for the kids' dinner and then four times a week I would prepare steak, rice and so on.

When it was Ed's evening to prepare dinner for the three kids, I would cheat on him. The kids would come home from school in the afternoon and let me take them to MacDonald's because they were hungry. I didn't believe that a salad for dinner would satisfy their hunger. This was especially true for Carmelo as he was raised in the Spanish way of life where meals are eaten slowly and enjoyed in a leisurely manner. He would tell me that lunch time at the school was about twenty minutes and he was not even half way through when time was up. When he tried to eat faster in order to finish his meal in the time allowed, he developed stomach ache. I agreed, therefore, to take them to McDonald's in the afternoon on the condition that they would finish their salad for dinner. I knew that if they didn't finish their food, Ed would suspect. This went on for many months until I could no longer live with the knowledge that either I cheat on my husband or Carmelo starved. So finally, I told Carmelo he had to go to another American family since he would only be in America for a year and he should experience real American living since we were not a normal American family. He begged to stay with us, even if it meant he would be deprived of barbecues, hot dogs, etc. However, I found another family who would give him a taste of the typical American life.

Family life
Both Ed and I took our responsibilities as parents seriously. We believed that it was a parent's job to raise the children and that the only way children could be raised effectively was for both parents to have a hand in it.

We saw to it that Betty and Eddie were always kept busy for that way we were assured that there would be no time for mischief. We would pay them for doing small tasks about the house and thus their allowance was earned rather than a right. We believed it gave them a realistic view of life. We also made sure that either Ed or I was with them so we could influence them appropriately in the many areas of life that children need to learn as they grow up.

We would make religious holidays and other holidays meaningful so that they had a character forming or informational aspect to them. This did not mean that there was no family fun – only that family fun was woven into all activities. When vacation time came, the children learned to plan as well as we did. They learned to contribute to being part of the family early on and I think that much of our present relationship was built brick by brick in their formative years.

Febes's faculty

At the end of the first year, our contracts were renewed but there were no salary increases for the next three years. I became a surrogate mother to my students. I passed out candies when I gave them exams in order to compensate for the hard work.

I spoke about ethics and was pleased to be working at a college where I could teach what I thought was important. I thought it vital that ethics was taught in each class so that students knew what was acceptable in their working environment and what was not. I spoke to them about my Chinese heritage and sometimes spent an entire lecture speaking about manners, kindness, the purpose of life, and the fear of God.

The story that my students tell me that they best remember is the Chinese axiom "Teach a man to fish and he will have fish on his plate for the rest of his life." I told them this story so that they would understand that I was teaching them to earn a living so that they would always be able to provide for themselves. I explained that they might like me better if I 'put fish on their plates', but if I did that, then in the future, their plates would be empty because I would not be there. I asked them, "When I'm gone, is that the time to learn to fish? Or will it be too late?" I would always tell my students, "I am teaching you to fish so that you will be independent and will not need to rely on anybody."

After our son, Eddie, graduated from college and moved to Los Angeles where he had a good job offer, I offered him some money. (Like all mothers, I was concerned that my child's needs be met.) Eddie told me, "Mom, you taught me how to fish and how to be independent and so you don't have to worry about me anymore. I can support myself now and you can spend your money to buy what you want for yourself." So Eddie learned his lessons well!

I also shared the Chinese philosophy of the eldest child. "When the eldest child begins to work," I told my students, "he sends home money so that his younger brothers and sisters can be educated." This meant, I told them, that once they were earning, it would be a good thing to send money to their alma mater so that scholarships could be provided for those that were less fortunate.

I told my students that I was preparing them, not only for work, but for their lives ahead. "What is your purpose in life? Why are you here? If you tell me that your purpose in life is to become a millionaire, then

Edward and Febes at
Commencement at Hillsdale
College in about 1978

Febes, Betty, Eddie and Edward
on Betty and Eddie's Graduation
day at Hillsdale in 1986.

THE JOY OF SURPRISE — Febes Facey, left, was chosen by the
Hillsdale College graduates as Professor of the Year. Her joy is
shared by College President George Roche and Donald R. Mossey.

Febes in the news somewhere
in the 80s!

Febes - the Mace bearer at
Commencement about 1994

Hope visiting
Hillsdale 1986

Connie and Carlos about 1986

Betty and Eddie in China, Summer 1985

Betty, Hope, Eddie, Connie and Febes on the way to China. Summer 1985

May 14, 2000.Betty graduates with a degree in Law at Loyola Law School in Los Angeles.

Febes (1962) on the left, Betty (1984) on the right, different times, different places, or is that true?

I will disown you. I do not know you," I said. "Life is more than money," I intoned repeatedly. In the years that followed, many chose to teach and many went on to become highly successful in various professions.

The question I asked myself throughout my life was, "What am I going to leave behind?" The answer for me was always that I contribute to the lives of others. In retrospect it seems to me that at some level, I always meant to be a teacher. Not everyone can be an empire builder; not everyone can discover or invent something that will change the course of history. That is left to the few. It is necessary to ask ourselves. "What will I leave behind?" The right time to ask this question is at the beginning of our lives. Of course, one can ask it as one gets older but it is better to ask it when one is beginning one's life, for that way, one's entire life can be spent fulfilling one's purpose.

So I asked it of my students, often. "What are you going to leave behind?"

I also emphasized how important it was to share. For example, a month before Thanksgiving and Easter, I would bring a canister to my classroom and ask my students to feed at least one poor person by donating $1.50. We would then send the money to missions and feel good that the money fed a few hundred people. It was important to remember others, I told them.

While Eddie and Betty were still at home, I would also announce to all my classes that if they were not going home for Thanksgiving, they could come to our house for dinner. I always cooked the biggest turkey I could find for I never knew how many people would come to our house.

In between it all, I taught accounting. I was tough and set tough exams. My students responded by working hard, by taking their studies seriously and by going on to become exemplary citizens and contributors. I told them that accounting was not an end in itself but a means to an end. I explained that one could be anything one wanted to be with an accounting background. In later years I was proud to note that some of my students had become doctors, others had become state representatives, one a sheriff and another even became the mayor of our town.

My students became my family and, often, it was reciprocal. One day a young man came to my office. His father had never been home, always at work or at play, but never with his family. On this day, this particular student told me that his father had asked him if he loved him. He replied, "How can I love someone I do not know?" He knew that he had hurt his father but that was the truth. His father told him that he was an ungrateful child. "After all that I have provided for you - a luxury house, a luxury car - this is the thanks I get?"

He answered his father, "Dad, I would rather live on the other side of the railroad tracks with a father I know than have all the luxuries and no father." He told his father, "It is too late for me. I never got to know you and it is impossible to love someone one does not know. But there is time for you to get to know my brothers and sisters and there is time for them to get to know you and love you. Why don't you begin with them?"

I was deeply touched that this student told me the story for it showed me how much I had become a part of their lives.

Another time, I was walking in the school cafeteria and saw one of my students smoking. I walked up to his table, took the pack of cigarettes lying on the table and put it in my pocket. When I turned my head to look at him, he had a questioning look in his eyes. So I gave him his cigarettes back and said, "Smoke yourself to death, " and continued along my way. Later that student went to Ed's office to give him the pack of cigarettes since I was already in the classroom. To my surprise, when he entered my classroom, he put $20.00 in the Thanksgiving can. He told me that the money was his 'beer and cigarettes' money for the weekend and he would not be tempted to smoke or drink if there was no money. I gave him a tap on his shoulder and told him that not only had he fed a few people but also improved his health. Years later that student was to tell me he never smoked again.

It was important to me that my students were prepared not only for their work but for all eventualities in their lives. This included many diverse areas such as their life purpose and manners. When, on cold winter days, they came to class wearing caps on their heads, I would say, "Please take off your cap. It's not raining or snowing inside." Once, a student told me that he had no time to brush his hair, to which I replied, somewhat flippantly, "It is alright to get up a few minutes earlier to comb your hair."

Being late was unacceptable. There was a young lady who was always late. I spoke to her and asked her to be on time. It didn't seem to make a difference and she continued to be late. I spoke to her again. Still, there was no change. So, one morning I looked around and saw that she was not there. I locked the inner class door and began to teach. Ten minutes after class began, there was a knock at the door. I looked through the glass window in the door and saw that it was the student. I ignored her and told my students to ignore her. I told them that she had to learn to be on time. I told them that when they worked for someone, they should not let their boss wait for them as they would be fired. The student continued to knock and knock. She knocked for quite a while. Then she went away. She learned her lesson well. She was never late again.

Four years later, my first accounting students were ready to graduate. As Hillsdale College was a liberal arts college, the big eight accounting firms did not seek out Hillsdale graduates and I set about to alter that state of affairs.

Ed and I had some money saved for the holidays and so we went off to Detroit for the day. I told Ed to take the children sightseeing while I went to the Renaissance Center where the offices of the big eight accounting firms were located. I went from one office to the other asking the receptionist if I could see the managing partner. The receptionist would ask me if I had an appointment. "No," I replied. I told myself that I had nothing to lose. All the receptionist could do was tell me that the partner wasn't in or that he was busy. Finally, I got to see one managing partner and spent most of the afternoon describing my methods of teaching accounting and telling him about Hillsdale College. I told him that our students were the best investment he could make for his company for they were well rounded. After a few hours, he gave me a check for two thousand dollars. I looked at it, thanked him and said, "I did not come here for money. I came to invite you to visit Hillsdale College to interview my students. You will never regret hiring our students." He did visit and as far as I know, there were never any regrets.

From that year on, my students were always employed. Soon, the big eight firms found their way to Hillsdale College at the end of each year and the college became synonymous with top quality accounting students.

Each year, my graduating students were interviewed by personnel from the big eight accounting firms. The interviewers were also delighted that I gave them cider and apples from a local orchard, a little taste of the country. Each year I would go to the orchards, pack buckets of apples, and prepare gallons of cider. It became a joke within the accounting community. When I met with colleagues from other universities for conferences, they always told me that most of the interviewers wanted to go to Hillsdale College because I gave them apples and cider. "Well, do likewise!" I teased them jokingly.

Pearl of wisdom

I believe that the most influential position on this earth is that of teacher. It is a teacher that influences lives. It is a teacher that directs the energies and efforts that can be put to either good or bad use. A teacher can influence many thousands of students during a twenty or thirty year teaching span. In later life, it is not famous ball players or well known actors and businessmen that are remembered when gazing back on one's life. It is one's teacher.

Is there a doctor in the house?

Eddie, was about seven years old and came to me with this question, "Mommy, how come our friend, Dr Rich, is the only one working? His wife does not work. Yet they have a sports car and a large house. You and Papa work so hard but we live in a rented house and have an old two door car that squeezes my sister and me in the back seat."

I said, "Sorry, kid, wrong kind of doctor!" I therefore want to forewarn the reader that I am writing the following based on observation, experience and common sense -not medical fact.

Observation

Man is supposedly the most intelligent member of the animal kingdom but he appears to be the most stupid when it comes to taking care of himself. If you observe an animal that is sick, it will not take any food or drugs. It will curl up in a corner and rest until it gets better. We, however, force people to eat and take drugs. I have always felt that every drug has its side effects (whether they are known to us or not).

We live in a highly industrialized society and in a generation of instant gratification. To live thus, we're subjected to many pressures during the day. Then, in order to drown the pressure, we reach for a cigarette, a cup of coffee or a cocktail. If we get sick, we stop at the corner drug store and pick up some drugs. We do not believe it necessary to suffer pain for we think we live in a society so advanced so that there is a cure for every ailment of the body. Then we end up taking yellow pills for this, green pills for that, and red pills for the other. I'm surprised we don't look like a walking medicine cabinet. And what do the pills do for us? It relieves the symptoms for a short time (it's a palliative) but not the cause of the pain. So, in addition to the original condition, we now have another layer of toxic intervention to deal with.

Adventures of a *Faster*

Just like many others, a hectic schedule affected my ability to care for myself adequately. There was never enough time to get everything done and by the time I came home in the late afternoon, I would have a cup of coffee to give me the energy to prepare meals for the family. In time, I grew even more tired, and started having coffee more frequently just to keep going. Not surprisingly, my general health began to decline.

In the summer of 1977, Ed earned some money for teaching an extra course. Using this, he had made a deposit for a two week stay at a health institute. It upset me at first for it would involve fasting and I had never fasted for more than twenty hours (during Lent). How was I going to fast for two weeks? I had been used to eating gourmet food and my body weight reflected that. However, feeling more tired than a dish rag, and with aches all over my body, I did not squawk a lot. It would be a good two weeks relief for me – no cooking or housework. I guessed it wouldn't be a picnic either but I thought that I might try 'the cure'.

Knowing that I would be without food for a period of time, I prepared for the fast by eating as if each day was a Mardi Gras. I felt like a convict who was going to the electric chair so each meal consisted of every food I could think of. I later found out (too late to be of any help) that the pre-fasting days (at least two days) should consist of fresh fruit and vegetables to ease the transition period from eating to fasting. Later, as I lay reading a book by Arnold de Vries (Therapeutic Fasting) I thought, "Woe is me! I must suffer the consequences."

I checked in on Sunday afternoon, July 10, 1977, after having a Western Omelet and coffee at the Holiday Inn in Cleveland. That was my last meal for a while. In my mind's eye, I clearly saw a sign at the door of the Natural Health Institute building saying, 'Abandon all hope, you who enter here!" (Of course, there was no such sign when I arrived.) I knew that the next two weeks were not going to be easy, not only for me, but for my family as well. My husband had to look after

Eddie (twelve years old), Betty (ten years old) and himself and he had never prepared meals for himself or the kids. I knew the kids would be on a vegetarian diet of fruit, nuts, and some raw goat's milk cheese. This made the parting more difficult. After they left, I put my clothes in the dresser and settled into bed. I asked myself if this was all there was to it. Night came and I did not sleep well.

The next morning I got up at six o clock to collect my urine specimen. The sample showed that my fast had started. I went back to bed, but at 8 am, the owner (he has a D.M. and a D.C. degree) came to take my blood pressure. I started having a spinning sensation and started throwing up.

The doctor diagnosed this as Meniere's Syndrome, a condition caused by an infection of the ear. It would hit me with a sudden impact that no carnival ride ever came close to imitating. I used to tell my kids that I got my rides free. The first day was the most miserable and I could not get out of bed for the first two days - not even to drink water.

When I looked back after the fast was over, I guess the best thing that happened was that I was able to continue the fast. I had heard that the first two days were the worst as a result of hunger pangs but I never did feel hungry. It was the spinning sickness that made it so terrible for me.

Every morning, the doctor would stop by to take my blood pressure. I was pleased to see my weight go down, at least a pound day.

However, at home in Hillsdale, Eddie and Betty were also losing weight. All told, for the two weeks, Eddie lost ten pounds, Betty lost five pounds, and Ed lost eight pounds. When I finally arrived home, they looked as if they had been through the same grinding machine that I had gone through.

I lost fifteen pounds and spent most of the day sleeping, reading and chatting with my room mate. The nights were the most difficult part of the twenty four hour day. I couldn't sleep. I turned to my right side, slept on my back, then to the left side, and reversed the routine over and over again. I became sore from lying down.

I had all kinds of unfounded fears like, "What if my digestive system digests itself?" or "How long will it take me to relearn to eat?" Or will I be as strong as I was before? Everything seemed to be in suspended animation. All these thoughts, of course, proved to be unfounded. They were part of my hallucinations. The days and nights all blended into one, for what can one do in bed except sleep, and sleep was difficult in coming.

Sometimes, I thought of all the Filipino and Chinese food that I longed to eat. It was worse than being in jail, for at least you get fed in jail. My hunger pangs were getting stronger and I was getting weaker. The good news was that the hungrier I became, the closer the day I would be able to break my fast.

Finally, the eleventh day arrived. I had freshly squeezed orange juice (the sweetest I have ever tasted), served in a small glass (half full) with an orange design pattern on the glass, and a straw and a beautiful napkin. I sipped it for ten minutes, never wanting it to be finished.

Three hours later, I received another half glass and three hours after that, watermelon juice. The next day, I had a thick shake of blended orange and pineapple for breakfast. Half an hour before lunch, I had a glass of carrot and apple juice and for lunch I had a fruit plate of papaya, cherries, grapes, nectarines, avocado, celery, carrot stick and romaine lettuce.

Later, I took a walk around the grounds before dinner – dinner was tossed salad without dressing or salt but had some steamed zucchini. The third day was the same as the second day. Finally, the days of penance ended and my family came to collect me on the fourteenth day. During my fasting days, I never failed to call home each day and my heart melted when I heard the kids voices, knowing that they were not being fed properly by their father. I also had some extraordinary experiences and I want to mention one.

It was about 4 a.m. on my ninth day of fasting and I awoke from sleep. I saw Jesus, dressed like the good Shepherd, holding a lamb at the foot of my bed. He did not say anything and I was not sure if I was dreaming or awake so I took my note book and wrote the following. "I am the lost sheep. Oh, merciful Jesus, my Good Shepherd, I love You, for much has been forgiven me. For I was one of the hundred sheep that strayed from the flock and you left the ninety nine to look for me and when you found me, you bent down and lovingly picked me up and hugged me whispering into my ear, 'Stray no more lest the big bad wolf find you before I do.' Thank you my Jesus, for being my good Shepherd."

When I woke later that morning, I thought about the event of the previous night and was unsure whether it was dream or real. I looked at my note book and saw that I had indeed written those words.

With the fasting experience behind me, I no longer dreaded another fast. In fact, I went back some years later and fasted for four weeks.

Miracles in the family

We had not been in Hillsdale very long when I had a rather unusual experience. It was after dinner on Thanksgiving, 1973, and I was sitting on my recliner reading a book. I was beginning to doze off. Then I heard my mother's voice calling me.

"Baby, Baby, I'm leaving now. Baby, I'm…" She spoke in our dialect and did not finish her sentence. I jumped out of my chair and asked Ed, who was sitting next to me, if he had heard Ma. He said no.

An hour later the phone rang and my sister, Connie, told me that Ma had passed away. It was about 9 a.m. Friday morning in the Philippines and in Hillsdale, it was 9 p.m. Thursday evening. Connie said that Ma had been sitting in her rocking chair on the balcony of Connie's house (where they had their pig farm) in Dadiangas, Cotabato. She had been talking to the servants when her head dropped down. The maids called my sister and they carried Ma to the car and then drove her to the hospital. On the way to the hospital, Ma opened her eyes and looked at Connie, but didn't say anything. It was about that time that I heard her voice.

I had always said to my mother, "Please, never leave me without telling me," and she was leaving me. I was her favorite child, the youngest of her children. For many years after her passing, I could not bring myself to look at a Mother's Day card.

Perhaps, the most intense experience for me was the one that follows. It was many years after my mother's death and each Mother's Day brought with it the grief that had been mine when she passed on. Realizing that I needed to move on, I prayed, "Ma, will you give me a sign? If you're already in heaven, please send me a white rose today."

Eddie, who had just received his driver's license, said to me, "Mom, I have enough money to take you out to dinner for Mother's Day." (He earned some money working odd jobs at the college.)

Betty said, "I want to go, too."

Eddie said that he couldn't afford to take her as well. So I volunteered to pay for Betty. Before the dinner, Eddie drove to a mall about forty miles away and went into a Sees Candy store. He bought a quarter pound of 'Turtles' in a box and gave it to me. I looked at it. There, on the top of the box was a white rose. Ma was in heaven!

I started crying.

Eddie, not understanding my tears, hastened to comfort me. "Mom," he said, "I'm sorry. I have no more money. I can only afford a quarter pound."

I then told him the reason for my tears.

Miracles through prayer

I was often reminded of the presence of my Lord by the miracles that took place from time to time in my life.

Once, Ed was invited to give a lecture at Notre Dame University in South Bend, Indiana, and I accompanied him. Indiana is about eighty miles from Hillsdale. After Ed's lecture, we were invited to dinner by our hosts. We accepted, unaware that a developing snow storm would soon engulf us. After dinner, we began the drive home, expecting to be back in Hillsdale within a few short hours.

Within half an hour, we were in the midst of a terrible snow storm. It was snowing hard and, unexpectedly, our car lost power. Consequently, we had no lights, no heater and the windshield wipers ceased working. The snow was coming fast. We looked for a place to stop but nothing was open -not even a gas station. It was as if we were the only two people on the planet.

I don't know about Ed but I was certainly scared. There is nothing more frightening than Mother Nature out in full force. The shenanigans of mankind pale in comparison. So I slipped into prayer, sure once more, that my God would find a way to take us to safety. Ed and I prayed for half an hour without pause. There was no relief in sight. The car became colder and colder and we were in fear that we would freeze to death. Then, for the next half hour, we sang songs, hymns, anything. Still, we found ourselves making such slow progress that we had traveled only a few miles. By the third half hour, I was silent. I didn't know what more to say or do. Then I began to cry. It was so cold, I thought we would die, that our lives were over. Ed said no, it wasn't over, we were still alive. He just kept driving and driving. We were the only ones on the road and we were freezing to death with no heat and lights.

I was worried what would happen to our two children if we didn't make it home. Long past midnight, we were still driving. The snow kept coming, harder and harder, and the harder it came, the slower we drove. We were so cold, so very cold. I don't think I will ever forget that cold. Eventually, in the early morning light, we arrived home. I climbed out of the car and looked at it. My eyes traveled down to the tires. Two of them were flat. We had been driving on the rims of the wheels.

To me, it was a miracle that we arrived home. So many things could have gone wrong. We might have died of hypothermia. Another car might have driven into us. We might have taken a wrong route, for in the falling snow, everything looked alike. Both Ed and I said prayers of gratitude, acknowledging that our safe arrival was an answer to prayer.

Of course, it wasn't the only time we were caught in the snow. Another time, there was a storm in Hillsdale and the snow was falling very heavily. Ed and I had already arrived at the College to teach our classes. The administration instructed the faculty to go home early. However, many of our students were already there so we decided to teach our classes.

When our classes had finished for the day, it was time to return home. By that time, the snow was about six feet deep and driving had become hazardous. Still, we had to get home for the children would be home from school. We drove slowly and eventually came to the turn-off for our home. We could not turn. We were boxed in by the snow. Ed decided that the only option was for him to walk home and fetch a shovel. This he did.

I waited for quite a while and eventually decided to walk home as well as he did not appear to be returning. On the way there, I met him trudging up the 'path' with the children in hand, each holding a shovel. The children were freezing by this time (Eddie was about ten and Betty eight). They climbed into the car for warmth.

At that point, a man with a snow plow came by and offered to make a way for the car but he wanted payment in cash in advance. Neither Ed nor the children brought any money. The man was adamant - either he was paid upfront or there would be no help from him.

At that moment, Betty said, "Look, Dad, I found $5.00 on the back seat!" Ed turned, and there it was - $5.00. Where did the five dollar bill come from? The children did not get that much money for allowance and neither Ed nor I sat in the back seat.

For me, it was another miracle.

Ongoing miracles

We eventually sold our home in the country as Ed and I had accepted positions at Nichols College in Massachusetts (then reconsidered and decided to remain at Hillsdale College). Hillsdale College offered us a house to rent near the College and we moved in. After we moved in, however, we discovered that it was not in good condition and it was somewhat uncomfortable, particularly during the summer as it had no air-conditioning. Ed and I were longing to have our own home again.

One hot and humid afternoon, not wanting to return home, I got in the car with the kids and drove around town since the car was air conditioned. It was about a week before classes began for the new semester and Ed was in his office. As we were driving around, we saw a house near the college with a 'For Sale' sign. The kids and I picked up Ed at the College and we all went to see the realtor. The realtor showed us inside the house and we liked it. The owner wanted to sell it on land contract and wanted a down payment of twelve thousand dollars.

We did not have that amount of money so it looked doubtful that we would be able to purchase it, much as we wanted it. I was hopeful, though, that a door would open. Sure enough, the next day, I received a letter from AOC with a check for twelve thousand dollars enclosed.

The check was from a TV distributorship company in Kansas City that Johnny owned. I was on the Board of Directors and had done some work for them during the Thanksgiving break and during the Christmas holiday period. When they had offered to pay me, I had declined, saying that Johnny had rewarded me well during the years and that it was a pleasure to be able to do some small thing for him.

The company sent me a check, anyway. I wonder what made them send me the exact amount I needed for the down payment at the exact time that I was looking for a house. Or is the question, "Who influenced them to send me the exact amount?" I cannot help but think that my heavenly Father had a hand in it.

We moved into our new house and we still live there. I have always felt that it is a very blessed house, for I remember that it was money that came to me in a miraculous way that enabled Ed and I to buy it.

Pearl of wisdom

I have come to believe that the many miracles of timing and practical assistance that have come to me are a result of constant prayer. I believe that this happens to all those who maintain this connection through daily prayer. I also believe that when we do not take care of that connection through daily contact, in some ways, our lives are not lived as well as they could be.

Father Paul finds a way

Father Paul Facey, Ed's Jesuit uncle priest, made it a point to go on retreat in Detroit even though he lived in Massachusetts. He did this so that he could come and stay with us for a few days so that he could be pampered by me! He would get, for example, freshly squeezed orange juice in the morning when he woke up and home cooked food in the evening.

One day we were driving to Detroit to take him to the retreat house and Father Paul was sitting in the front seat with Ed, who was driving. I was sitting in the back seat of the car. Ed played a tape comparing traditional Catholic teaching to modern Catholicism. Father Paul told Ed in his soft voice to please turn it off but Ed ignored his request. As I was watching Father Paul from the back seat, I saw him remove his hearing aid. I started laughing and Ed turned his head and asked me why I was laughing. I told him to look at what Father Paul had done. Ed got the point!

Family visits to the Philippines

From time to time, I would fly back to the Philippines to visit family. Sometimes, it would be for a family event like a funeral, other times I simply went home to be with family. Often Hope accompanied me, and once both Betty and Ed came along. We would stay with Carlos and Connie.

They owned one of the biggest pig farms in the Philippines. It was located in the southern part and the islanders described it as the closest thing to paradise. Not only did Carlos and Connie own large tracts of land, but the house they had built on the land, was enormous. To add interest, there was a Japanese tea house in the middle of a man made lake where big goldfish and carp swam. Guests slept on the floor on a mat in typical Japanese style and the balcony was covered with hanging flowers like orchids, etc. The fragrance was always beautiful, sometimes overpowering.

Aside from the pigs (about five thousand), there were also cattle, chickens and fish in the ponds. If I wanted to have grilled fish, I would tell the man in charge of the fish pond and he would build a fire with charcoal and drain a portion of the pond. All the fish would be squirming and I would point out the one that I liked. He would pick it up, clean it, and then barbecue it for me. In the early morning, accompanied by a maid, I would visit the different pig houses which consisted of a hospital, maternity wards, breeding pens, and so on. Along the way, I would pick a ripe papaya from the tree and eat it as we walked. There were many different fruit trees – mangoes, guavas, jackfruit to name a few.

When Connie and Carlos gave a party, they invited the entire town. They would roast about twenty pigs for *lechon*, split several steer in half and barbecue them, and serve chicken, fish and anything else one could think of. And it all came from the farm!

Eventually, Connie and Carlos sold the pig farm in the Philippines and started one in China. This came about because China wanted to open its borders to Western business. It was virgin territory, however, and they did not particularly trust Western business interests. Fortunately for Carlos, one of his best friends from his revolutionary days, Liang, remained in China and became more influential in the Communist Party, eventually being named Governor of Guangdong Province.

Liang contacted Carlos and asked him to act as a liaison, identifying contractors to construct housing units and implement the latest animal husbandry techniques developed in the West. Carlos identified a company called Sand Livestock Systems in Columbus, Nebraska as the partner who would construct the units. They built the first pilot farm in Guangdong province, and it performed satisfactorily. With this experience, Sand Livestock Systems was awarded contracts to build dozens of these swine confinement units throughout China. These were fairly sizeable contracts and Carlos received commissions from Sand for each one that was built.

At that time, the Chinese government ruled that any new start up business would be a joint venture with the government. The government would take half as they provided the land, and the other half would belong to the private investor. Connie and Carlos shared their investment with an American from Nebraska so that they owned a quarter of the business.

Whenever a plane arrived in Guangchow, the passengers were hundreds of sow from Denmark. These pigs were for breeding and were white and lean with an extra rib. They were treated like gold and whenever anyone went into the piggery, there was quite a procedure. One had to put on a white jacket and pants, rubber boots, and then go through ultra violet light to prevent carrying diseases to the pigs. There was also special feed imported from Canada.

The large, wooden family home was surrounded by fruit trees, with a place to house the servants as China did not permit people to be employed as servants. So Connie and Carlos brought their two maids from the Philippines.

History also appeared to repeat itself there. Once more, a member of my family turned out to introduce a flush toilet (most people went to outhouses). They realized this when a guest experienced an unexpectedly hot butt when he flushed the toilet. The engineer must have been inexperienced and connected a hot water pipe rather than a cold one.

Hillsdale College

In the years that followed my students' graduation, many of them sent funds and it was always the accounting department that provided more scholarship money than any other department. One young woman has been sending me a Christmas card each Christmas for more than twenty years and inside it, without fail, is a $10,000 check for Hillsdale College.

At reunions, many students have found their way to my door and shared with me the influence I had on them. They tell me stories that I told them which I have long forgotten but which have had a profound effect on their lives. I have always felt blessed that God has used my abilities to touch the lives of others.

Sometimes, I have met past students in faraway places - in Las Vegas at a casino, in Hawaii on the beach, in Hong Kong while shopping. It has always been a wonderful surprise and given me a feeling of connection to the world around me.

As the reputation of Hillsdale became synonymous with high quality accounting graduates, so members of the big eight accounting firms began to donate money. Even Sears Roebuck, not an accounting firm, gave $1000.00 to Hillsdale College to be awarded to the most outstanding professor. Imagine my amazement and delight when I was awarded it. It was unexpected but heart felt. I was awarded 'Professor of the Year' three times.

Yet I wonder how much of this was possible without the constant prayer to my Father in heaven. I kept up the heavy workload only with His assistance. Did I ever doubt that He was there?

In all, I taught at Hillsdale College for twenty one years and then retired in 1994. During that time, the accounting department expanded to between thirty to forty students graduating each year. After I left, two full time professors succeeded me but the workload was such that the accounting major was once more closed for a time. In 2004 four students graduated in accounting as a result of changes in the requirements for the CPA exam.

Looking back at my time as a professor, I spent a full thirty years of my life teaching. The one thing I miss most in my retirement is my relationship with my students.

Ironically, in all my years of teaching, I never lost my fear of it. I was always aware of how my every word and action would affect the way a student turned out. I still believe that, though it might not be initially apparent, our words affect those around us. Each word is like a wave rippling through a lake, setting off a chain reaction that cannot be stopped.

Perhaps, the thing that I tried most to exemplify was that hard work would always achieve the desired result. Talent and ability play a part, but more than anything, if someone wants something, it is hard work and persistent effort that will bring about the desired goal. More than anything, it does not matter what we do, so long as we do it. Hard work is something to be proud of, not ashamed of.

My life has been about hard work, prayer, loving God and helping my neighbor.

New beginnings

It is traditional for Hillsdale College to give a retirement party for outgoing professors and at the end of the college year in 1994, it was my turn as well as that of an English professor, Dr. Robert Rice. It was attended by more than 200 people – the President of the College, faculty members, former students and families of the retiring professors. Connie and Carlos came from Manila. Hope and Joseph (Joe Jr.) were there and so were Betty and Eddie. It was a good party, filled with moments of sadness because that part of my life was drawing to a close.

A business deal - with God!

When I was still teaching, I had made a deal with our Lord. I promised that if I didn't get sick and miss a day of class, I would be all His after I retired. Naturally, when retirement finally came, so did temptation. There were many offers of work, for example, I was offered, amongst others, the position of Dean of the Graduate School of Business and a position as a consultant in Asia.

As I was praying about these offers, I asked the Lord which offer I should accept. The answer wasn't quite what I was expecting. "You made a deal with Me. You have a roof over your head and enough money to buy food. What more do you want? I want you to be free for Me to use if I so desire." I apologized and committed to keeping my promise. After all, He had done His share.

One time, Eddie came to Hillsdale from Los Angeles to talk me into accepting a consulting position in Asia. He told me that a friend of his had asked him if he knew someone with the same qualifications that I had. Eddie told him that he knew someone with exactly the qualifications he was looking for (not because I was his mother, but because the job demanded the experience and qualifications I already had). Eddie realized that if he asked me by phone I would decline and so he flew home. I told him about my deal with the Lord, that I would not work for pay, and he understood.

Another time, a vice president of a company in Hillsdale was taking an accounting course via computer. Since he needed help, his wife (a friend of mine) asked me to help him. So I did. After he passed the course with an A, he wanted to pay me and I told him that I did not work for pay. When I told our priest about it, the priest said that if the vice president wanted to pay me, the money could be donated to the Church instead, so that is what happened.

While I have had no formal position with Hillsdale College since I retired, I have continued to be involved with the affairs of the school. In 2003, nearly nine years after my retirement, I received the Alumnae Award for service to the school. Throughout the years of my retirement, students have called on me at home and I have been delighted at the way that they have steered themselves through this life.

Traveling days

Travel continued to enrich my life during retirement. From about 1995, Connie and Carlos arrived each summer to spend three or four months with their daughters, Jean and Joy, as well as Hope and me. Jean is married to Lucio SayGan, a surgeon and has one daughter and four stepdaughters (Lucio is a widower). Joy is married to Dave Gilmore, and the couple has two children.

Connie and Carlos had purchased a big van and so we spent the summer traveling from the east coast to the west coast, and from north to south. We went to Atlantic City, New York City, Cleveland, Mount Rushmore, the Dakotas, Yellowstone, Las Vegas, Reno, San Diego, San Francisco, Houston, Nebraska and Florida, and so on. Connie's two other children, Pauline (the only one not married) and Boboy, and two maids would come as well.

Traveling in the van was a unique experience. Boboy would drive and Pauline would sit in the front seat taking care of the music (CDs and tapes). The next row of seats would be taken by Connie and Carlos with the television between them. I would sit in the third row watching television with a maid on each side. They would massage me and feed us all while we were traveling.

As we joked and shared stories, I slowly became aware that I needed to speak to Connie about her spiritual journey, the one that would be opening for her when she took her leave from this earth. I also became aware that she had not prepared a will and so in February, 1997, I decided to travel to Manila and spend two months with her. Hope came, too.

It was the Chinese New Year and for the traditional celebration. Carlos, Connie, Hope and I boarded a hydrofoil and made the 45 minute journey to Macau, the island next to Hong Kong. Once there, we spent a few days at Hotel Lisboa, a casino hotel on the island. It was almost exclusively in the hands of organized crime and so there were prostitutes, known as 'White Russians', that took rooms at the hotel.

Chinese people love to gamble but it was illegal in Hong Kong so many made their way to the Hotel Lisboa which was the only casino on the island. In those days, it generated more gambling revenue per square foot of casino floor space than any other casino in the world. The place had a tremendous buzz and it was difficult to focus on any one thing for long.

On the second or third night there, there was a birthday party which all guests could attend. There were twelve different courses, each one served after the previous one was finished. The dinner went on for three hours and then it was time for the show which we had arranged to go to. The next move was for everybody to go to the restroom before the show. We formed a line with Hope next to me. As Hope and I spoke, I opened the door to the rest room and did not see the step in front of me. (I thought it was level all the way.) I toppled over and hit the other side of the room, landing flat on my back. It happened so quickly that I cannot recall the exact details except to say that the pain was instantaneous and I couldn't move.

Dark clouds, silver linings

An ambulance from the Macau hospital came to fetch me. After the x-ray, the doctor told me that I had broken both my clavicle and my ankle. He wanted to perform surgery. I shuddered. "No," I said, "If there is to be surgery, then I will return to the United States."

"You can't do that," interrupted Connie. "Who will look after you?" She had a point. "We can go to China and you can be attended by a doctor there." So, after I was discharged, Connie, Carlos, Hope and I boarded yet another hydrofoil and made our way to Connie and Carlos's house in China.

Once we arrived, we made the three or four hour journey to the hospital. The doctor told me that I would need to be there at least a month and that he would need to see me three times a week. The difficulty was that the doctor left promptly at twelve noon each day and it would be difficult for us to arrive in time as it was such a long car ride.

In China, medical treatment costs about a dollar a visit as visits are subsidized by the country. Doctors are paid a salary and are not motivated to be on call any longer than their allocated hours. However, our interpreter and guide would give the doctor some dollars and he would wait for us at the hospital until we arrived.

We would start out early in the morning and arrive at noon. There were five of us in the car. The front seat would have the driver and the interpreter. Hope, Pauline and I would be in the back seat. When we arrived, the doctor and the nurse would be waiting for me. He would unwrap my bandages, poke around, then rewrap me. I could not move so Connie employed a maid to look after me. The maid would cut the meat on my plate, help me to take a bath and change my clothes. I lived like this for a month.

The accident gave me time to speak to Connie about our Lord and about our Catholic faith. We spent long hours speaking and at times we touched in a way that brought us even closer than we already were. There came a time when I understood that even when bad things happen (my clavicle never did heal properly), good things can come through them. Connie and I were both more at peace, knowing that each would go to a better place when we left this earth. Now it was time to document the untidy details of money after she departed. I broached the subject of her preparing a will so that there would be no quarrelling among their kids after she and Carlos were gone. She looked at me blankly

"What money?" asked Connie. "We have no money."

I looked at Carlos and he said, "What is she talking about?" For Carlos and Connie were rich and respected. Connie always tried to minimize that they were rich. I used to kid her that even if all the banks failed, she would always have some in reserve.

I was to see Connie and Carlos again in the summer when they came to America for their annual vacation. Again, we traveled. It was the last time I saw either of them alive and well.

The call

Just before Christmas, 1997, I received a call to come to Manila as Connie was in a coma in a hospital. Hope, Jean, Joy and I took the first flight available. When we arrived, we found that Carlos was in hospital as well. This was not because there was anything wrong with him, but because when they took Connie to the hospital, they discovered that there was nobody to look after Carlos so they took him along, too. He was given the room next to Connie.

As we drove to the hospital, Pauline told us that Connie had been to the doctor the previous day for pain. He had given her some pain pills and she had taken them. She started hallucinating that night and saw non-existent dogs and cats under her bed and in her room. She was taken to the hospital that night. The next morning she turned blue and it was feared that she was dying. However, the medical staff were able to resuscitate her, even though they were unable to prevent her from going into a coma. We arrived at the hospital and I went to see Connie first, then I slipped in to see Carlos.

"Baby, I'm so happy that you're here. We'll have a big reunion." Carlos said to me. Yet we never did speak much, for shortly after that Carlos's leg turned black as a result of diabetic complications.

At Christmas some fifty members of the family gathered at the hospital to have their *Media-noche* meal after the midnight Mass at the hospital. Both Connie and Carlos were transferred to the intensive care unit downstairs. It was a subdued meal. It was like the Exodus in the Bible, a last meal between people who meant a great deal to each other. We were eating from paper plates. The maids had covered the beds with plastic in the two rooms that Carlos and Connie had vacated and spread all the food on the covered bed. This was perfectly acceptable in the Philippines. On New Year's Eve, the family once again gathered at the hospital. Again, there were about fifty of us.

Then, on the January 6, 1998, the doctor amputated Carlos' leg below the knee. He never recovered from the operation and on January 8, 1998, as I was sitting next to Carlos on his bed, I saw that he was struggling. I held his hand and said to him, "Brother, you don't have to worry about us anymore. We will be okay. You can go now." I watched the IV going down, down, down to zero. There was a tear that formed in his eye and slowly it rolled down his cheek, and then he passed from this world to the next. Carlos never knew that Connie was in the room next door to him.

Hope was with Connie. I went to her and told her that Carlos had just passed.

Carlos was an important man in Manila and so he had a high profile funeral. As was the Chinese custom, he was cremated. His body lay in church for one week with people constantly calling to pay their last respects. As family, it was our duty to feed the hundreds of people who came, so we made an arrangement with all the nearby restaurants to serve the people (we paid the bills).

It was an old Chinese custom to build a large paper house with Barbie dolls on the balcony waving good-bye to the departed one. They also built big paper airplanes and burned gold paper money. This was done for twenty four hours per day for seven days for the Chinese believe the dead need money and other material goods in the next world. At his funeral, the house, the dolls, the plane and the money were all burned while he was being cremated. This meant that all these things went with him.

On January 15, unable to remain in Manila much longer, and with Connie's condition showing no change, I returned to Hillsdale. I returned again on the May 31, 1998 for her funeral. Her body, too, lay in a coffin in a church for a week. Next to her was the urn containing Carlos' ashes.

After Connie passed from this world, her children built a mausoleum in the cemetery to house the remains of both their parents. It has become a tradition that each Sunday, the family goes to the mausoleum to have a picnic. Before their deaths, the family had gathered each Sunday for a picnic – so the tradition continues.

Neither Connie nor Carlos ever knew that the other had passed on. I still can't figure out whether it was a curse or a blessing.

Another call

Those were not the only deaths in the family that year. Estela (Momita), Marino's widow, went to spend a holiday with Hope in Vancouver. It was Estela and Hope's habit to rise early in the morning so they could spend the day chatting. Their friendship had commenced during childhood years when they were classmates in high school. Hope called me in Michigan and told me that she was having breakfast alone since Momita was still sleeping. An hour later, Hope called me again to tell me the same thing. After a while, Hope became concerned and went to the bedroom and found that Momita was not breathing anymore.

Estela had passed during the night. Hope did not know what to do as Momita's two children who lived in Vancouver, were out camping. She called me and I immediately flew to Vancouver to be with her and help with funeral arrangements.

Stones

In the thirty years I taught, I never had any serious illness. My retirement has been different. I've had cataract surgery for my eyes and one fine day, after waking up in terrible pain and calling on my doctor, I discovered that I had gallstones. If I stayed in Hillsdale, Ed did not want to see me lose a gallbladder and favored a return to Dr. Scott in Ohio. I thought my case now required surgery and decided to go to Los Angeles and be with my daughter, Betty, who worked at Cedars Sinai Hospital. Betty arranged for the best anesthesiologist to attend to me and when he came to prepare me for surgery (at ten in the morning) he said to me, "I heard that you asked for me."

I looked at him blankly for a moment, then replied, "No, my daughter asked for you. She works here and she has heard that you are the best." That was the last I remember. I awoke in a room full of flowers – like a florist shop! They were from friends and family, from the staff at the hospital, and far too many to count. I loved the experience. It was good to feel cared for.

At six the following morning, the nurse woke me and told me to get out of bed. My sister, Hope, who stayed with me in my room in the hospital, was watching eagerly what I would do. The nurse wanted me to get out of bed but my body definitely was not in agreement. The nurse remained firm and held my IV as I made my way to the bathroom. It wasn't as bad as I thought it might be so I told the nurse that since I was up, I did not want to return to bed and would check out. Later the doctor came to see me to sign my dismissal papers. "How many stones did I have?" I asked him.

He gave me a strange look. "I gave up counting," he replied.

Stepping out

On the way home that same day, I collected a Petri dish containing the stones. They looked like chocolate chips. I counted. There were forty. Anyone of them could have caused an obstruction somewhere in my body and I would have left this world. Another reprieve, I thought. Recovery was swift and two days later, we all went to the San Diego Zoo and had a good time. Animals soothe the soul. They remind us that we are all part of a much bigger picture.

Pearl of wisdom

At that time, I asked the Lord to take me home because I felt I had already served my purpose here but He said, "Not yet, I need more beggars to beg for alms daily for the salvation of souls."

I thought about my life, then, and decided that life is like going to school daily then final exams arrive, and if we pass, then graduation. These final exams are not graded the way some professors grade their students – by curve. It is not a comparison as to how well we did in comparison with another. No, it is God's standard and that is the one we will be measured against. Did we ask for forgiveness when we sinned? Did we live our lives and embrace His precepts? At the end of this life, after the finals, there will be graduation day.

It is both our last day here, and our first day there. From there, we will begin a new life. So, my thought was that if God asked something from me, the answer would always be, "Yes, yes, yes, my Lord. Here I am - your number one beggar who is not afraid or ashamed to beg if I can only help to bring souls to Thee."

Sisters in retirement

Hope is my only surviving sister. At 85, she is quite remarkable. She still socializes with the American Association of University Women, although at this point, most of the members are considerably younger than she is.

We speak daily by email and visit on occasion. She is very fit for her years.

Up to about five years ago, she used to go hiking with various groups regularly. Then, she had her first health scare (her heart) and went to see a doctor. She was seventy nine years old. That was the first time she had been to see a doctor and he gave her some tablets. She has always been blessed with good health and energy, and has remained much younger than her years.

Hope and I regard religion in different ways. She feels that it is through kindness that we interact with each other, and that it is the kindness we show to others, that reflects our connectivity with God.

Hope lives a happy life, has two wonderful children, Joe and Marie who live relatively nearby and visit her often. They go to the beach at times, and other times just stay home to chat. She has no financial worries, many wonderful friends and is part of an organization that gives meaning to her life. She can get up when she wants to, spends her days in any way she pleases. She feels that she has a wonderful life and is truly blessed.

Hope sees her life in three stages. The first is the one in which she was a second class citizen living in China and the Philippines. She had no rights. The second was her life with her husband and her children in America. Her marriage was happy and she and Joe lived a good life. The third part of her life came about after Joe died in 1967. It was then that she became the person who lay hidden so many years. She went to university to educate herself and then she taught. She finally became the person she really was. Those were the years that she did many things, including write Haiku and poetry. She always loved English literature and, now, she reads more than ever.

In her own way, Hope takes life as seriously as I do. She continues to live the very best way that she can. Time waits for no man. She once said to me, "For me, the epitaph will simply be that I was dealt a hand of cards, played it the best way I knew how, and in the process, lived a very good life."

Daily bread

In my retirement, I have a routine. I still wake up around five or so. It has been a lifetime habit as I was never able to sleep for more than four or five hours each night. I feed Frosty Sr, our dog, and then make all Ed's meals for the day. It's a lengthy procedure. For breakfast I cut up watermelon, honeydew melon and cantaloupe. Then I grind up pecan nuts, cashew nuts and some almonds. (He will have these later in the morning with a glass of romaine lettuce, carrots, celery and tomato juice.) Then I prepare his lunch and dinner and refrigerate them. For lunch, it is papaya, mango, pear, apple, avocado and

Romaine lettuce. For dinner, it is blended salad of Romaine lettuce, cucumber, zucchini, avocado and sweet corn. And then my day is my own.

Prayer comes first. I spend the next two hours in prayer and then there's email to check. Then to church at about eleven each morning to set up the altar for Mass. Mass is an important part of my life. After that, I'll meet with friends for lunch. Sometimes it will be the local Burger King and other times a local restaurant. I will usually eat half a sandwich for lunch and take home the other half for dinner. At other times I will eat a much bigger meal. I seldom cook dinner these days. Instead, if I'm in the mood for Chinese food, I will pick up some from a local Chinese restaurant. After supper I watch the news with Ed while he is having his dinner. Always at some time during the day, I will read from a devotional book like *Divine Intimacy* for a few hours or, perhaps, the *Magnificat* or some other book. Currently, I'm reading a book on Mother Teresa sent to me by the bishop. In it, Mother Teresa said that she is just a pen in God's Hands.

Somewhere around ten, we make our way to bed. Ed will massage my back while we listen to his tapes (usually controversial topics).

With each passing day, I know that I'm getting closer to my final Home. I look back and know that my life has been a grand tapestry with the Lord and Mother Mary always at my side.

Often, I have been asked how it was that growing up in an environment where 19th century traditions still reigned and where women were in submission to men, that I made the decisions I did, and having made them, managed to act on them.

I believe firmly that anybody can do anything that they desire. It just depends on whether they're willing to do the hard work. I think that if the work is done then the results will follow. I was always willing to do the hard work.

People tend to blame their misfortunes on their parents, on their race, or that they were underprivileged from the start – whatever excuses they can manufacture. I believe we make a grave error of judgment when we teach people to believe that they have not succeeded because the system doesn't allow them to succeed.

What really counts is the individual and his or her motivation – especially in America. In other countries, it is who you know that gets you there. In America, it is what you know and what you want to be. For a long time, I didn't know what America was all about but now I know. It's about shooting for the stars and nobody stopping you. You can just go on and on – as high as you want! I have had to work very hard here. But I have not minded it, for what is work?

Work is the thing we do that gives us reason to live. Work is the way in which we find out who we are. Work is the way in which we move from achievement to achievement. Work is the thing that enables us to survive. Work is the mechanism by which we grow from babyhood to adulthood, and from adulthood to wisdom-hood. Work is also the means by which we leave behind something of value. Without work, we cannot be much. Nor can we fully appreciate what we have.

Work is many things. Work is motherhood. Work is helping others to become who they are. Work is focusing on one's health. Work is taking responsibility for outcomes. Work is doing the things we don't like to do but have to do because if we don't do them, then we or others might suffer. There will be many failures but it is not how many times we fall down, it is how fast we pick ourselves up after the fall.

Above all things, work induces creation. Without work, there can be no new creation, and without new creation, we would become stagnant and when we are stagnant we move towards death. In that way, I believe that work is life.

In America, we are free to a certain extent. I think too many do not value or understand freedom.

Where I grew up, I never had a life of my own. I was always under the thumb of my elders but not so in America. For instance, if I received a letter, it was already opened and read by someone else before I saw it.

In those countries in which people do not have freedom, they do not understand what freedom is, for they have lived with it for a lifetime and taken it for granted. It is only when one has never tasted it and later finds it, that one begins to understand how precious, how valuable freedom is. Today, most in the free world grow up with freedom as a right so they seldom realize that without freedom, they could not live the lives they do.

There are two factors that made me aware of freedom initially. The first was my sister, Hope, whose rebellious ways led her to marry a Filipino employed by the US army. After she moved to the US, she changed and I picked up those changes where I was.

The second factor was my mother's marriage to my father. I did not want to be a chattel in my husband's household. My sister had a man to herself. I think these motivations were subconscious and in the moment that I saw the advertisement for the Fulbright scholarship, some mental arithmetic within my mind put the pieces together.

After I had attended Stanford, I had a far better understanding of another way of life. So, when I returned to the Philippines, although the opportunity for marriage was there, my thoughts were tumultuous. How could I ever live in the Philippines again – or marry a Chinese man?

All of these things speak of a yearning for freedom. I didn't know it in my childhood but somewhere there must have been a moment of understanding of what freedom was and I silently longed for it.

I often think of the story of the French poodle, manicured and molly coddled, sitting on a throne-like chair. "Look at me," he says to the stray dog passing by, "you cannot sit like me on this chair."

"No," says the stray dog, "But I can bark if I like."

I respect and value freedom. Yet, in my marriage, I have tied myself to a man. This has been no modern marriage. It has been traditional in many ways. Both Ed and myself believe that marriage is for life, that it is for better or for worse, that to be unfaithful is to do the unthinkable, that to go to sleep with anger acting as a wedge between us, is sinful. Ed and I do not agree on some things, the most rift-forming being religion and his diet. Yet, if I insisted that he change then I remove from him his freedom to be who he chooses to be.

So how have I coped in a marriage where there has been deep disagreement? How have I coped with a life that has taken me from cowering beside a wooden cart in a 120 mph typhoon in a remote island culture to being an Asian woman teaching students in the United States?

I believe.

I believe in God.

I believe in God, the Father Almighty, Creator of heaven and earth; and in Jesus Christ, His only Son, our Lord: Who was conceived by the Holy Ghost, born of the Virgin Mary, suffered under Pontius Pilate, was crucified, died, and was buried. He descended into hell: the third day He arose again from the dead. He ascended into heaven, sitteth at the right hand of God, the Father Almighty; from thence He shall come to judge the living and the dead. I believe in the Holy Ghost, the Holy Catholic Church, the Communion of Saints, the forgiveness of sins, the resurrection of the body, and life everlasting. Amen.

If I have but one lesson to share with anyone who reads this book, it is this: If you truly love and have enough faith in Jesus, you will never be alone. Despair and loneliness will no longer be part your life. He is always there for you, for He loves each one of us. Is there any better love than this? When I am afraid, I know that my faith is weak for when my faith is strong, I don't fear anything. I know that my Lord is with me and will see me through.

It is this belief that has carried me through my life. In times of desperation, I have prayed and had my prayers answered. In times of fear, I clung to the thought of my Holy Father. In times of sorrow, I comforted myself with the promises of the Almighty. Yet, I have also praised my Father in joy, giving thanks for what He has given me and been confident that my joys are as much His concern as my sorrows. I have to carry my Cross and follow Jesus each day for I know that He loves me, even though I don't always do the right thing. He died for me. So how can there be any doubt that He loves me? My only doubt is whether I love Him as I should.

The many miracles in my life have assured me that there is life after death; that life is far more than just this experience we have on this planet.

It is with my hand in His that I have trodden every step that I have taken. I firmly believe that when we open our hearts to the Father, then He directs our steps in a way so that we can live happily. Sometimes, those steps are difficult but in every journey there are patches where the road is not smooth.

Sometimes it seems that the road we are on could not possibly be the one that we should have chosen. I believe that each choice we make affects the path we're on. Eventually, the sum of all our choices bring us to a place we may or may not recognize. If it is not what we would have wished for, then we must recognize that we have made our bed and we must lie on it. With the freedom to choose comes the responsibility to choose wisely. Nobody else is to blame for our choices. We suffer the consequences of our choices. At these times, it is important that we have faith and trust in God. We may not see Him, but I am convinced that He is there for I feel Him often. I am also convinced that prayer, humble and superstitious instrument that some may consider it, is a phone line to the Lord of all that is visible and invisible.

Perhaps, the meld of these two cultures, my extensive travels, the differences between an early 20th century lifestyle and a modern world have contributed to my viewpoint.

Pearl of wisdom

Sometimes I think it's time to do an about face, time to turn back the world to the way it used to be, time to return to religious status quo of previous times. And sometimes I think that this may well be our last chance to do so.

In our world today, it seems that the acceptable thing is to pick our religion to suit our lifestyle. Choosing a religion that endorses our lifestyle is akin to choosing to read a book so as to support our opinion in regard to that lifestyle.

New religions and different understanding of current religions are growing in numbers. It's a smorgasbord to pick and choose what suits one. The problem is that there's no broccoli, no carrots, no spinach - nothing that gives us the nutrition we need. Dessert might taste good but it doesn't give us eternal Life.

The pearl of wisdom that I gained from this was that what one likes is not necessarily what we need to flourish.

Oneness

I believe that all people are equally important. We have different functions and can do different things but one person is not more expendable than another. We see this in Mother Nature. If we remove one species (no matter how irrelevant we think that species is), the eco system is harmed in ways we only discover much later. We all have a place on this earth. And we are all able to do the things we were designed to do.

Many have asked me throughout my life how I can be so convinced that my faith is justified. I only have to look at the many miracles of timing and provision in my life for me to know that something else (or someone else) is at work.

Important aspects of life

In my retirement, I visit my sister, Hope, in Vancouver, Washington, as well as my children, Betty and Eddie, in Los Angeles. I am always open to new experiences and encourage those around me to spread their wings, regardless of their age and occupation.

An aspect of my life that has become even more important to me now, is my faith in God. With each passing day, I am becoming more and more aware of how important our *invisible* lives are.

Often, I hear my Lord speaking to me. He says to me, "I have given you everything, down to the last drop of My Blood. I continue to give you everything but I will never remove your free will from you. You are always free to choose." Like everyone else, I am human. Yet I am moved to reply to my Lord and say, "The more you give us, the more we take You for granted. We are selfish, focusing only on our own needs."

I spend my days going to Mass. I spend time in prayer. I spend time giving to those around me. Time is the most precious commodity I have to give. I give it freely for if I am focused on taking much, then I cannot be instrumental in giving. It is in giving that we receive and it is in giving that our lives become worthwhile. It is through this worth that we develop an awareness of our place in the world.

Would I have changed any of the decisions I made in the past? Would I have remained in Manila? Would I have married someone else? Would I have preferred to stay in New York to play a high profile part?

No. My life has been spent in service to others. That was my choice and, if at times, there were difficulties, then that is no different from anyone else. We all have difficulties

As I look at each patch of the tapestry that has been my life, I cherish it. There is the patch of 'Ed' and the patch of 'Eddie'; there is the patch of 'Betty' and the patch of 'my sisters'. There is the patch of 'my brother' and the patch of 'my journey to America'. There is the patch of 'my time at Stanford' and the patch of 'New York University'. There are many, many patches. They make my tapestry rich and colorful, warm and meaningful. Soon I will go to meet my Lord but I do not hesitate. It has been a good life and my vast family is closely connected and prosperous.

As my days are reduced to a precious few, I try to have my bags packed, ready for when the good Lord calls me, for each day brings me closer to Him! Being an accountant, I know where the best investment is, where interest and dividends are out of this world. I look forward to meeting with Him and walking with Him throughout eternity. Finally, I know what that pearl is: It is spending eternity with the Ruler of the Universe in a time and place of beauty, peace and goodness.

Sometimes when I wrote in those note books, something would come to me. One day, I saw my life as a parcel on this earth and I saw that death would come. I knew that I would like my soul to be wrapped up, with the following address:

To God, my Maker,
Destination: Heaven.
From Febes Tan Facey.
Your Beloved Child.

The message would read: Return to Maker. Please accept. This box contains the old, broken, and wretched body and soul of Thy beloved creature for repair and renewal and hope of life everlasting with Thee! Warranty has not expired for it is an unlimited warranty. Thank you my dearest Lord.

© Dr. Febes Tan Facey, Michigan, 2006

Made in the USA
San Bernardino, CA
12 November 2019